John Denison Baldwin

Ancient America, in notes on American archaeology

John Denison Baldwin

Ancient America, in notes on American archaeology

ISBN/EAN: 9783741155420

Manufactured in Europe, USA, Canada, Australia, Japa

Cover: Foto ©ninafisch / pixelio.de

Manufactured and distributed by brebook publishing software (www.brebook.com)

John Denison Baldwin

Ancient America, in notes on American archaeology

ANCIENT AMERICA,

IN

NOTES ON AMERICAN ARCHÆOLOGY.

By JOHN D. BALDWIN, A.M.,
AUTHOR OF "PRE-HISTORIC NATIONS."

WITH ILLUSTRATIONS.

NEW YORK:
HARPER & BROTHERS, PUBLISHERS,
FRANKLIN SQUARE.

PREFACE.

The purpose of this volume is to give a summary of what is known of American Antiquities, with some thoughts and suggestions relative to their significance. It aims at nothing more. No similar work, I believe, has been published in English or in any other language. What is known of American Archæology is recorded in a great many volumes, English, French, Spanish, and German, each work being confined to some particular department of the subject, or containing only an intelligent traveler's brief sketches of what he saw as he went through some of the districts where the old ruins are found. Many of the more important of these works are either in French or Spanish, or in great English quartos and folios which are not accessible to general readers, and not one of them attempts to give a comprehensive view of the whole subject.

Therefore I have prepared this work for publication, believing it will be acceptable to many who are not now much acquainted with the remains of Ancient America, and that some who read it may be induced to study the subject in the more elaborate volumes to which I refer. It has grown out of a short and hastily prepared series of papers on American Archæology, written for a newspaper, the Worcester Spy. While writing them, I took more notice than ever before of the lack of such a work as I have endeavored to make this; and the brief papers, when printed, engaged so much more attention than I expected, and brought me so many letters from different parts of the country, that I was induced to take up the subject again, with a view to supplying this want. Having at hand the necessary materials, I began anew. The result is now presented to the public.

My purpose has not allowed me to make the book larger, as I could have done easily, by introducing elaborate descriptions of all the known works of the Mound-Builders, and of all the ruins and other traces of the ancient people of Mexico, Central America, and Peru, which have been examined and described. I have sought to show accurately their character and extent, without attempting a more particular and extended description of every monument and relic of the Ancient American civilization than this purpose seemed to require. The work is a summary, a kind of hand-book with notes and comments; but I have aimed to make it comprehensive and complete. The suggestions in regard to the history of Ancient America, furnished by such old Mexican and Central American books as have been preserved, seem to me no less important than the ruins themselves; therefore this portion of the subject has been kept in view; and I have also reviewed the various theories and suggestions put forward from time to time to explain the ancient American civilizations, adding suggestions of my own.

The pictorial illustrations used are all from original drawings, and are believed to be authentic, although in some cases (such as No. 5, for instance) restored views are given, and the works are shown as they were, probably, when the lines and surfaces were new and unworn. A few of the illustrations were prepared for this work, but most of them have been copied from drawings made by Mr. Squier and others for the work of Squier and Davis on the Mound-Builders, published by the Smithsonian Institution; from Catherwood's views of the Mexican and Central American ruins; and from drawings made originally for the work of Von Tschudi and Rivero, and for Harper's Magazine, on Peru. The two full-page illustrations of Mitla are from Desiré Charnay's photographs; the others were drawn by Von Temski. The restored Pueblo edifice and its ground plan have been drawn in accordance with the suggestions and sketches of Lieutenant Simpson; the other views of Pueblo ruins were made originally for Harper's Magazine.

In the Appendix will be found several papers which have only an indirect connection with the main topic;

but as Ancient America covers all time previous to the discovery by Columbus, they may not be deemed out of place. Materials for the paper on "Antiquities of the Pacific Islands" came to me from the Pacific World while I was preparing the others. The discovery of the Pacific is so intimately connected with the discovery of America, that this paper would not be out of place even if the Mexican and Peruvian traditions did not mention that a foreign people communicated with the western coast of America in very ancient times.

WORCESTER, MASS., *November*, 1871.

CONTENTS.

		Page
I. ANCIENT AMERICA.—THE MOUND-BUILDERS		13
Works of the Mound-Builders		14
Extent of their Settlements		31
Their Civilization		33
Their Ancient Mining Works		43
II. ANTIQUITY OF THE MOUND-BUILDERS		47
How long were they here?		51
III. WHO WERE THE MOUND-BUILDERS?		57
Not Ancestors of the Wild Indians		58
Brereton's Story		62
American Ethnology		65
Who the Mound-Builders were		70
IV. MEXICO AND CENTRAL AMERICA		76
Their Northern Remains		77
The "Seven Cities of Cevola"		85
Central Mexico		89
The great Ruins at the South		93
V. MEXICO AND CENTRAL AMERICA		103
Palenque		104
Copan and Quiragua		111
Mitla		117
An Astronomical Monument		122
Ruins farther South		123
The Ruins in Yucatan		125
Mayapan		127
Uxmal		131
Kabah		137
Chichen-Itza		140
Other Ruins		144
VI. ANTIQUITY OF THE RUINS		151
Distinct Eras traced		155
Nothing perishable left		156
"The Oldest of Civilizations"		159
American Cities seen by Tyrians		161

A 2

Contents.

VII. WHENCE CAME THIS CIVILIZATION? 165
   The "Lost Tribes of Israel" 166
   The "Malay" Theory 167
   The Phœnician Theory 171
   The "Atlantic" Theory 174
   It was an original Civilization 184

VIII. AMERICAN ANCIENT HISTORY 187
   The Old Books not all lost 189
   The Ancient History sketched 197
   The Toltecs our Mound-Builders 200
   Some confirmation of the History 205

IX. THE AZTEC CIVILIZATION 207
   The Discovery and Invasion 209
   The City of Mexico 211
   The Conquest 213
   Who were the Aztecs? 216
   They came from the South 217

X. ANCIENT PERU 222
   The Spanish Hunt for Peru 223
   The Ruins near Lake Titicaca 226
   Other Ruins in Peru 237
   The great Peruvian Roads 243
   The Peruvian Civilization 246

XI. PERUVIAN ANCIENT HISTORY 257
   Garcillasso's History 258
   Fernando Montesinos 261
   His Scheme of Peruvian History 264
   Probabilities 268
   Conclusion 272

APPENDIX 277
   A. The Northmen in America 279
   B. The Welsh in America 285
   C. Antiquities of the Pacific Islands 288
   D. Deciphering the Inscriptions 292

LIST OF ILLUSTRATIONS.

		Page
1.	Gateway at Labna.................................	*Frontispiece*
2.	Great Mound near Miamisburg.....................	16
3.	Square Mound near Marietta......................	18
4.	Works at Cedar Bank, Ohio.......................	19
5.	Works in Washington County, Mississippi.........	20
6.	Works at Hopeton, Ohio..........................	22
7.	Principal Figures of the Hopeton Works..........	23
8.	Graded Way near Piketon, Ohio...................	25
9.	Great Serpent Inclosure.........................	29
10.	Fortified Hill, Butler County, Ohio............	30
11.	Stone-work in Paint Creek Valley, Ohio.........	35
12.	Work on North Fork of Paint Creek..............	36
13.	Ancient Work, Pike County, Ohio................	38
14.	Work near Brownsville, Ohio....................	38
15.	Works near Liberty, Ohio.......................	39
16.	Work in Randolph County, Indiana...............	40
17. 18.	} Vases from the Mounds......................	41
19.	Ancient Mining Shaft...........................	45
20.	Pueblo Ruin at Pecos...........................	80
21.	Modern Zuni....................................	81
22.	Ruins in the Valley of the Gila................	83
23.	Pueblo Building restored.......................	87
24.	Ground Plan of the Building....................	88
25.	Arch of Los Monjas, Uxmal......................	98
26.	Arch most common in the Ruins..................	100
27.	Casa No. 1, Palenque...........................	107
28.	Casa No. 9 (La Cruz), Palenque..................	108
29.	Great Wall at Copan............................	112
30.	Ruins at Mitla.................................	116
31.	Great Hall at Mitla............................	118
32.	A ruined "Palace" at Mitla.....................	119
33.	Mosaic Decoration at Mitla.....................	120
34.	Great Mound at Mayapan.........................	127
35.	Circular Edifice at Mayapan....................	129
36.	Casa del Gobernador, Uxmal.....................	131
37.	Ground Plan....................................	132
38.	Two-headed Figure at Uxmal.....................	133

List of Illustrations.

	Page
39. Decorations over Doorway, Uxmal	134
40. Ground Plan of Las Monjas, Uxmal	136
41. Ruined Arch at Kabah	139
42. Casa Colorada, Chichen-Itza	141
43. Great Stone Ring	143
44. Great Mound at Xcoch	145
45. Bottom of an Aguada	146
46. Subterranean Reservoir	147
47. Plan of the Walls of Tuloom	148
48. Watch-tower at Tuloom	149
49. Specimen of Inscriptions on Stone	190
50. Specimen of the Manuscript Writing	197
51. Ancient Masonry at Cuzco	227
52. Ruins of a "Temple" on the Island of Titicaca	228
53. Ruin on the Island of Titicaca	229
54. Ruin on the Island of Coati	231
55. Monolithic Gateway at Tiahuanaco	233
56. Remains of Fortress Walls at Cuzco	234
57. End View of Fortress Walls at Cuzco	235
58. End View of Walls at Gran-Chimu	238
59. 60. } Decorations at Chimu-Canchu	239
61. Edifice at Old Huanuco	239
62. Ground Plan of the Edifice	240
63. "Look-out" at Old Huanuco	240
64. Ruins at Pachacamac	243
65. Peruvian Copper Knives	249
66. Copper Tweezers	249
67. Golden Vase of Ancient Peru	251
68. Ancient Peruvian Silver Vase	251
69. Ancient Peruvian Pottery	253
70. Ancient Peruvian Pottery	253

ANCIENT AMERICA.

I.

THE MOUND-BUILDERS.

ONE of the most learned writers on American antiquities, a Frenchman, speaking of discoveries in Peru, exclaims, "America is to be again discovered! We must remove the veil in which Spanish politics has sought to bury its ancient civilization!" In this case, quite as much is due to the ignorance, indifference, unscrupulous greed, and religious fanaticism of the Spaniards, as to Spanish politics. The gold-hunting marauders who subjugated Mexico and Peru could be robbers and destroyers, but they were not qualified in any respect to become intelligent students of American antiquity. What a select company of investigators, such as could be organized in our time, might have done in Mexico and Central America, for instance, three hundred and fifty years ago, is easily understood. In what they did, and in what they failed to do, the Spaniards who went there acted in strict accordance with such character as they had; and yet we are not wholly without obligation to some of the more intelligent Spaniards connected with the Conquest.

There are existing monuments of an American ancient history which invite study, and most of which might, doubtless, have been studied more successfully in the first part of the sixteenth century, before nearly all the old books of Central America had been destroyed by Spanish fanaticism, than at present. Remains of ancient civilizations, differing to some extent in degree and character, are found in three great sections of the American continent: the west side of South America, between Chili and the first or second degree of north latitude; Central America and Mexico; and the valleys of the Mississippi and the Ohio. These regions have all been explored to some extent—not completely, but sufficiently to show the significance and importance of their archæological remains, most of which were already mysterious antiquities when the continent was discovered by Columbus. I propose to give some account of these antiquities, not for the edification of those already learned in American archæology, but for general readers who have not made the subject a study. My sketches will begin with the Mississippi Valley and the regions connected with it.

THE MOUND-BUILDERS—THEIR WORKS.

An ancient and unknown people left remains of settled life, and of a certain degree of civilization, in the valleys of the Mississippi and its tributaries. We have no authentic name for them either as a nation or a race;

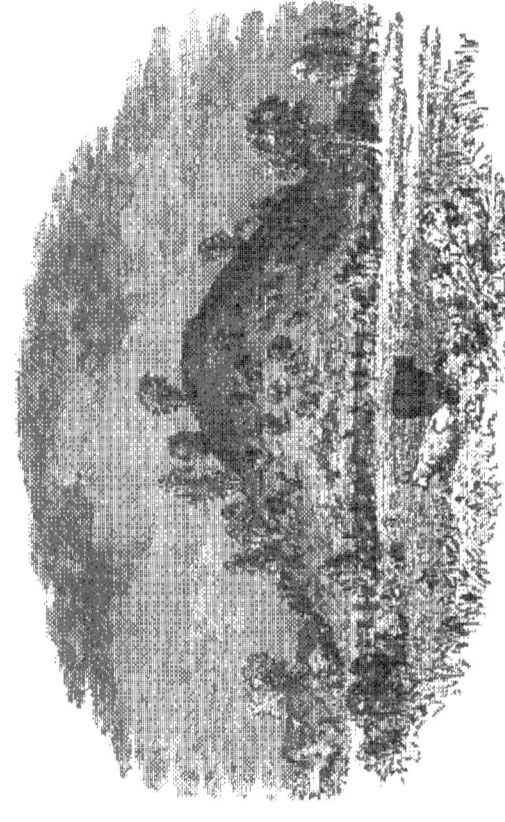

Fig. 2.—The Great Mound, near Miamisburg.

therefore they are called "Mound-Builders," this name having been suggested by an important class of their works.

Prominent among the remains by which we know that such a people once inhabited that region are artificial mounds constructed with intelligence and great labor. Most of them are terraced and truncated pyramids. In shape they are usually square or rectangular, but sometimes hexagonal or octagonal, and the higher mounds appear to have been constructed with winding stairways on the outside leading to their summits. Many of these structures have a close resemblance to the *teocallis* of Mexico. They differ considerably in size. The great mound at Grave Creek, West Virginia, is 70 feet high and 1000 feet in circumference at the base. A mound in Miamisburg, Ohio, is 68 feet high and 852 feet in circumference. The great truncated pyramid at Cahokia, Illinois, is 700 feet long, 500 wide, and 90 in height. Generally, however, these mounds range from 6 to 30 feet high. In the lower valley of the Mississippi they are usually larger in horizontal extent, with less elevation.

Figure 2 represents the great mound near Miamisburg, Ohio, which may be compared with a similar structure at Mayapan, Yucatan (Fig. 34). Figure 3 shows a square mound near Marietta, Ohio.

There have been a great many conjectures in regard to the purposes for which these mounds were built, some of them rather fanciful. I find it most reasonable to believe that the mounds in this part of the continent were

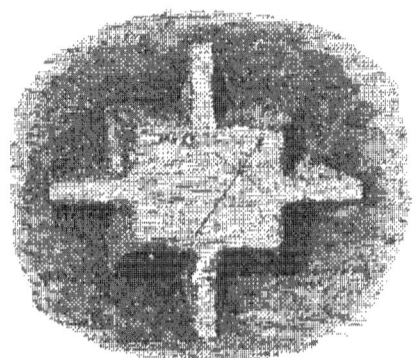

Fig. 1.—Square Mound, near Marietta.

used precisely as similar structures were used in Mexico and Central America. The lower mounds, or most of them, must have been constructed as foundations of the more important edifices of the mound-building people. Many of the great buildings erected on such pyramidal foundations, at Palenque, Uxmal, and elsewhere in that region, have not disappeared, because they were built of hewn stone laid in mortar. For reasons not difficult to understand, the Mound-Builders, beginning their works on the lower Mississippi, constructed such edifices of wood or some other perishable material; therefore not a trace of them remains. The higher mounds, with broad, flat summits, reached by flights of steps on the outside, are like the Mexican *teocallis*, or temples. In Mexico and Central America these structures were very numerous. They are described as solid pyramidal masses of earth, cased with brick or stone, level at the top, and furnished with ascending ranges of steps on the outside. The resemblance is striking, and the most reasonable explanation seems to be that in both regions mounds of this class were intended for the same uses. Figure 4

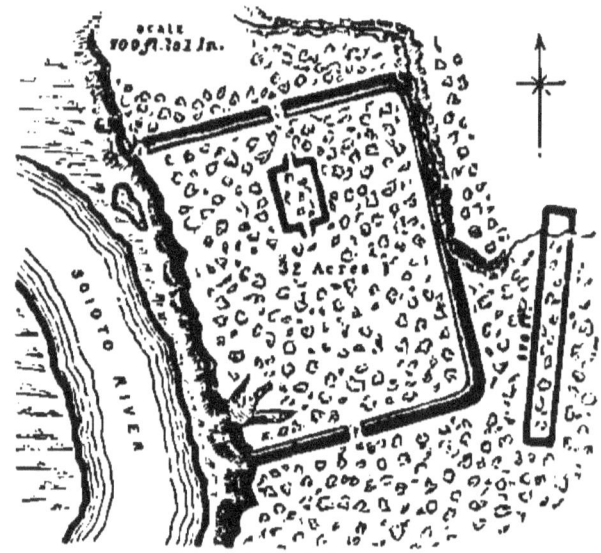

Fig. 4.—Works at Cedar Bank, Ohio.

shows the works at Cedar Bank, Ohio, inclosing a mound. The mound within the inclosure is 245 feet long by 150 broad. Figure 5 shows a group of mounds in Washington County, Mississippi, some of which are connected by means of causeways.

Another class of these antiquities consists of inclosures formed by heavy embankments of earth and stone.

20   *Ancient America.*

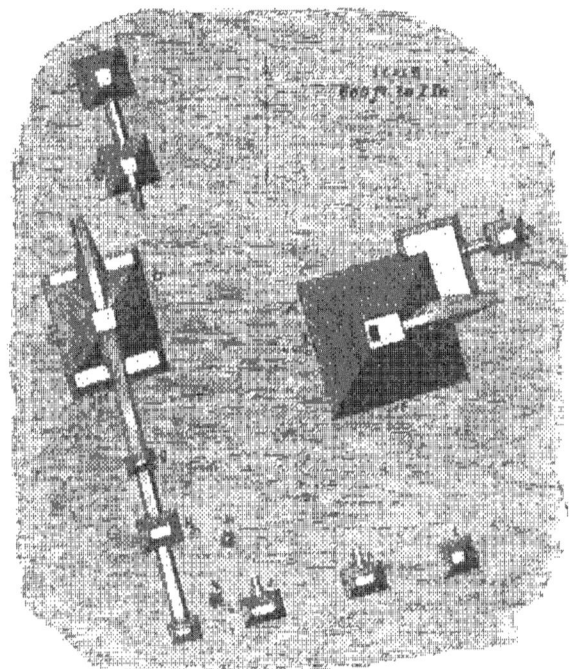

Fig. 5.—Works in Washington County, Mississippi.

There is nothing to explain these constructions so clearly as to leave no room for conjecture and speculation. It has been suggested that some of them may have been intended for defense, others for religious purposes. A portion of them, it may be, encircled villages or towns. In some cases the ditches or fosses were on the inside, in others on the outside. But no one can fully explain why they were made. We know only that they were

Fig. 6.—Works at Hopeton, Ohio.

prepared intelligently, with great labor, for human uses. "Lines of embankment varying from 5 to 30 feet in height, and inclosing from 1 to 50 acres, are very common, while inclosures containing from 100 to 200 acres are not infrequent, and occasional works are found inclosing as many as 400 acres." Figures 6 and 7 give views of the Hopeton works, four miles north of Chillicothe, Ohio. Combinations of the square and circle are

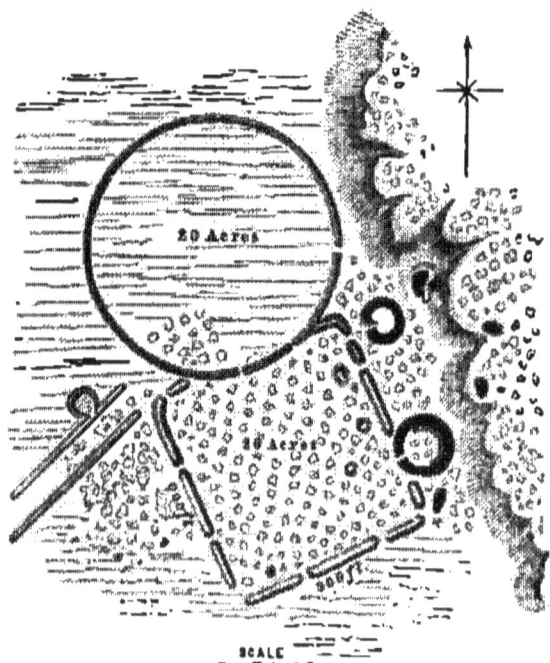

Fig. 7.—Principal Figures of the Hopeton Works.

common in these ancient works, and the figures are always perfect. This perfection of the figures proves, as Squier and Davis remark, that "the builders possessed a standard of measurement, and had a means of determining angles."

About 100 inclosures and 500 mounds have been examined in Ross County, Ohio. The number of mounds in the whole state is estimated at over 10,000, and the number of inclosures at more than 1500. The great number of these ancient remains in the regions occupied by the Mound-Builders is really surprising. They are more numerous in the regions on the lower Mississippi and the Gulf of Mexico than any where else; and here, in some cases, sun-dried brick was used in the embankments.

One peculiarity at the South is, that while the inclosures are generally smaller and comparatively less numerous, there is a greater proportion of low mounds, and these are often larger in extent. Harrison Mound, in South Carolina, is 480 feet in circumference and 15 feet high. Another is described as 500 feet in circumference at the base, 225 at the summit, and 34 feet high. In a small mound near this, which was opened, there was found "an urn holding 46 quarts," and also a considerable deposit of beads and shell ornaments very much decomposed. Broad terraces of various heights, mounds with several stages, elevated passages, and long avenues, and aguadas or artificial ponds, are common at the South. Figure 8 shows the remains of a graded way of this ancient people near Piketon, Ohio.

Fig. 2.—Graded Way near Piketon, Ohio.

At Seltzertown, Mississippi, there is a mound 600 feet long, 400 wide, and 40 feet high. The area of its level summit measures 4 acres. There was a ditch around it, and near it are smaller mounds. Mr. J. R. Bartlett says, on the authority of Dr. M.W. Dickeson, "The north side of this mound is supported by a wall of sun-dried brick two feet thick, filled with grass, rushes, and leaves." Dr. Dickeson mentions angular tumuli, with corners "still quite perfect," and "formed of large bricks bearing the impression of human hands." In Louisiana, near the Trinity, there is a great inclosure partially faced with sun-dried bricks of large size; and in this neighborhood ditches and artificial ponds have been examined. In the Southern States these works appear to assume a closer resemblance to the mound work of Central America.

The result of intelligent exploration and study of these antiquities is stated as follows: "Although possessing throughout certain general points of resemblance going to establish a kindred origin, these works nevertheless resolve themselves into three grand geographical divisions, which present in many respects striking contrasts, yet so gradually merge into each other that it is impossible to determine where one series terminates and another begins." On the upper lakes, and to a certain extent in Michigan, Iowa, and Missouri, but particularly in Wisconsin, the outlines of the inclosures (elsewhere more regular in form) were designed in the forms of animals, birds, serpents, and even men, appearing on the surface of the country like huge *relievos*. The embankment of an irregular inclosure in Adams County, Ohio, is described as follows by Squier and Davis, Mr. Squier having made the drawing of it for the work published by the Smithsonian Institution:

"It is in the form of a serpent, upward of 1000 feet in length, extended in graceful curves, and terminating in a triple coil at the tail. The embankment constituting this figure is more than 5 feet high, with a base 30 feet wide at the centre of the body, diminishing somewhat toward the head and tail. The neck of the figure is stretched out and slightly curved. The mouth is wide open, and seems in the act of swallowing or ejecting an oval figure which rests partly within the distended jaws. This oval is formed by an embankment 4 feet high, and is perfectly regular in outline, its transverse and conjugate diameters being respectively 160 and 80 feet. The combined figure has been regarded as a symbolical illustration of the Oriental cosmological idea of the serpent and the egg; but, however this may be, little doubt can exist of the symbolical character of the monument."

Figure 9 gives a view of this work.

No symbolic device is more common among the antiquities of Mexico and Central America than the form of the serpent, and it was sometimes reproduced in part in architectural constructions. One of the old books, giving account of a temple dedicated to Quetzalcohuatl, says, "It was circular in form, and the entrance represented the mouth of a serpent, opened in a frightful manner, and extremely terrifying to those who approached it for the first time."

On the Ohio and its tributaries, and farther south,

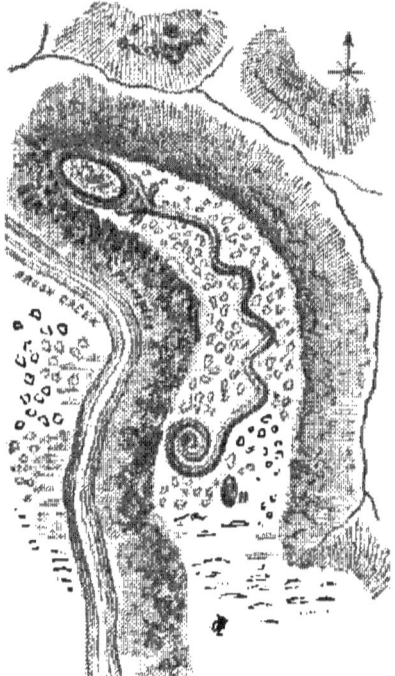

Fig. 9.—Great Serpent, Adams County, Ohio.

where the mounds are numerous, the inclosures have more regular forms; and in the Ohio Valley very often their great extent has incited speculation. At Newark, Ohio, when first discovered, they were spread over an area more than two miles square, and still showed more than twelve miles of embankment from two to twenty feet high. Farther south, as already stated, the inclos-

30   *Ancient America.*

ures are fewer and smaller, or, to speak more exactly, the great inclosures and high mounds are much less common than low truncated pyramids, and pyramidal platforms or foundations with dependent works. Passing up the valley, it is found that Marietta, Newark, Ports-

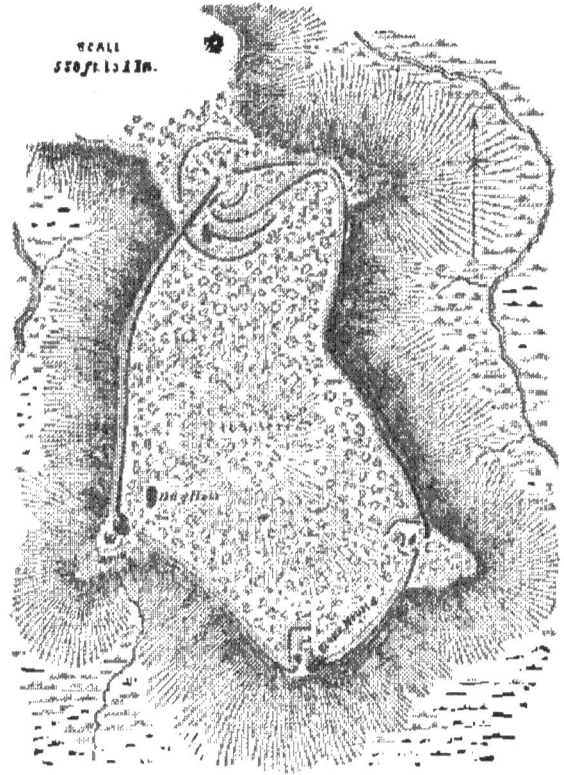

Fig. 10.—Fortified Hill, Butler County, Ohio.

mouth, Chillicothe, Circleville, Ohio; St. Louis, Missouri, and Frankfort, Kentucky, were favorite seats of the Mound-Builders. This leads one of the most intelligent investigators to remark that "the centres of population are now where they were when the mysterious race of Mound-Builders existed." There is, however, this difference: the remains indicate that their most populous and advanced communities were at the South. Figure 10 shows a fortified hill in Butler County, Ohio.

Among those who have examined and described remains of the Mound-Builders, Messrs. Squier and Davis rank first in importance, because they have done most to give a particular and comprehensive account of them. Their great work, published by the Smithsonian Institution, must be regarded as the highest authority, and those who desire to study the whole subject more in detail will find that work indispensable.

EXTENT OF THEIR SETTLEMENTS.

Careful study of what is shown in the many reports on these ancient remains seems plainly to authorize the conclusion that the Mound-Builders entered the country at the South, and began their settlements near the Gulf. Here they must have been very numerous, while their works at every point on the limit of their distribution, north, east, and west, indicate a much less numerous border population. Remains of their works have been traced through a great extent of country. They are found in West Virginia, and are spread through Michigan, Wisconsin, and Iowa to Nebraska. Lewis and Clarke reported seeing them on the Missouri River, a thousand miles above its junction with the Mississippi; but this report has not been satisfactorily verified. They have been observed on the Kansas, Platte, and other remote Western rivers, it is said. They are found all over the intermediate and the more southern country, being most numerous in Ohio, Indiana, Illinois, Wisconsin, Missouri, Arkansas, Kentucky, Tennessee, Louisiana, Mississippi, Alabama, Georgia, Florida, and Texas.

This ancient race seems to have occupied nearly the whole basin of the Mississippi and its tributaries, with the fertile plains along the Gulf, and their settlements were continued across the Rio Grande into Mexico; but toward their eastern, northern, and western limit the population was evidently smaller, and their occupation of the territory less complete than in the Valley of the Ohio, and from that point down to the Gulf. No other united people previous to our time can be supposed to have occupied so large an extent of territory in this part of North America.

It has heretofore been stated that remains of this people exist in Western New York, but a more intelligent and careful examination shows that the works in Western New York are not remains of the Mound-Builders. This is now the opinion of Mr. Squier, formed on personal investigation since the great work of Squier and Davis was published.

THEIR CIVILIZATION.

It is usual to rank the civilized life of the Mound-Builders much below that of the ancient people of Mexico and Central America. This may be correct, for the remains as they now exist appear to justify it. But if all the ancient stone-work in Central America, with its finely-carved inscriptions and wonderful decorations, had disappeared in the ages before Europeans visited this continent, the difference might not appear to be so great; for then the Central American remains, consisting only of earth-works, truncated pyramids, pyramidal foundations, and their connected works made of earth, would have a closer resemblance to works of the Mound-Builders, to those especially found on the lower Mississippi. On the other hand, if we now had in the Ohio and Mississippi Valleys remains of the more important edifices anciently constructed there, the Mound-Builders might be placed considerably higher in the scale of civilization than it has been customary to allow.

It can be seen, without long study of their works as we know them, that the Mound-Builders had a certain degree of civilization which raised them far above the condition of savages. To make such works possible under any circumstances, there must be settled life, with its accumulations and intelligently organized industry. Fixed habits of useful work, directed by intelligence, are what barbarous tribes lack most of all. A profound change in this respect is indispensable to the beginning of civilization in such tribes.

No savage tribe found here by Europeans could have undertaken such constructions as those of the Mound-Builders. The wild Indians found in North America lived rudely in tribes. They had only such organization as was required by their nomadic habits, and their methods of hunting and fighting. These barbarous Indians gave no sign of being capable of the systematic application to useful industry which promotes intelligence, elevates the condition of life, accumulates wealth, and undertakes great works. This condition of industry, of which the worn and decayed works of the Mound-Builders are unmistakable monuments, means civilization.

Albert Gallatin, who gave considerable attention to their remains, thought their works indicated not only "a dense agricultural population," but also a state of society essentially different from that of the Iroquois and Algonquin Indians. He was sure that the people who established such settlements and built such works must have been "eminently agricultural." No trace of their ordinary dwellings is left. These must have been constructed of perishable materials, which went to dust long before great forests had again covered most of the regions through which they were scattered. Doubtless their dwellings and other edifices were made of wood, and they must have been numerous. It is abundantly evident that there were large towns at such places as Newark, Circleville, and Marietta, in Ohio. Figures 11 and 12 give views of works on Paint Creek, Ohio.

Their agricultural products may have been similar to many of those found in Mexico; and it is not improb-

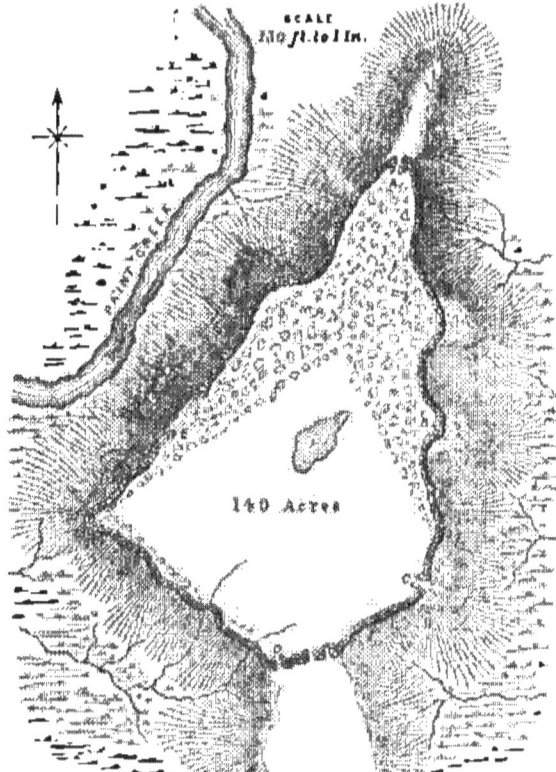

Fig. 11.—Stone-work in Paint Creek Valley, Ohio.

able that the barbarous Indians, who afterward occupied the country, learned from them the cultivation of maize. Their unity as a people, which is every where so manifest, must have been expressed in political organization, else it could not have been maintained.

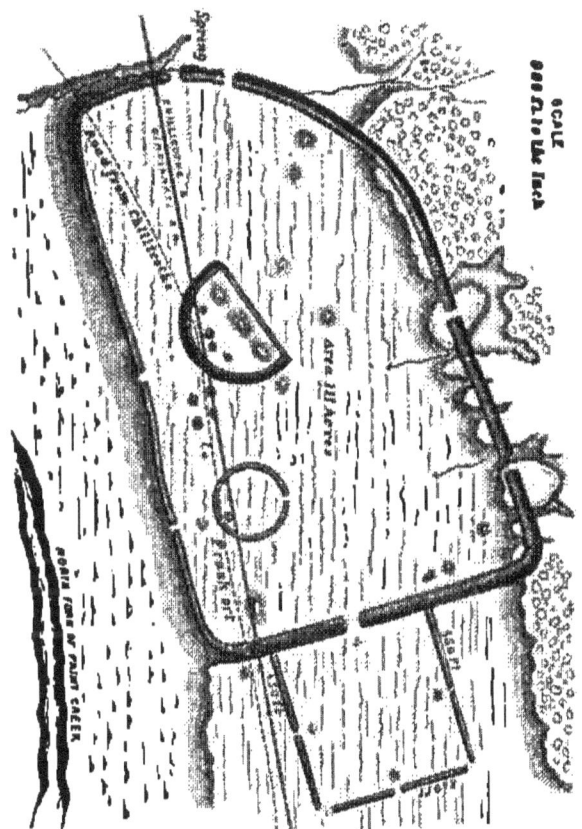

Fig. 12.—Work on North Fork of Paint Creek.

In the details of their works, and in manufactured articles taken from the mounds, there is evidence of considerable civilization. For instance, it has been ascer-

Fig. 13.—Ancient Work, Pike County, Ohio.

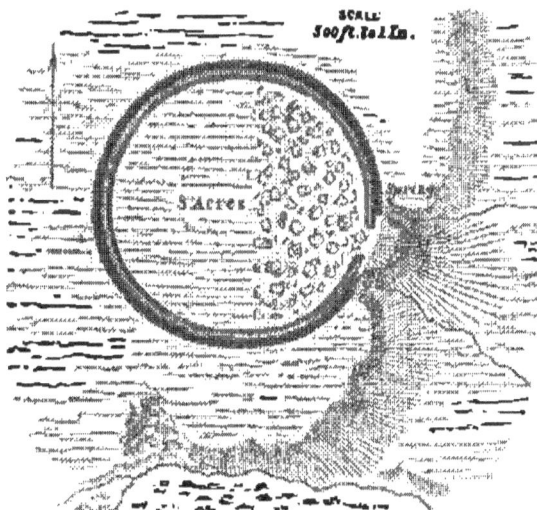

Fig. 14.—Elliptical Work near Brownsville, Ohio.

tained that the circular inclosures are perfect circles, and the square inclosures perfect squares. They were constructed with a geometrical precision which implies a kind of knowledge in the builders that may be called scientific. Figures 13, 14, 15, 16 show some of the more

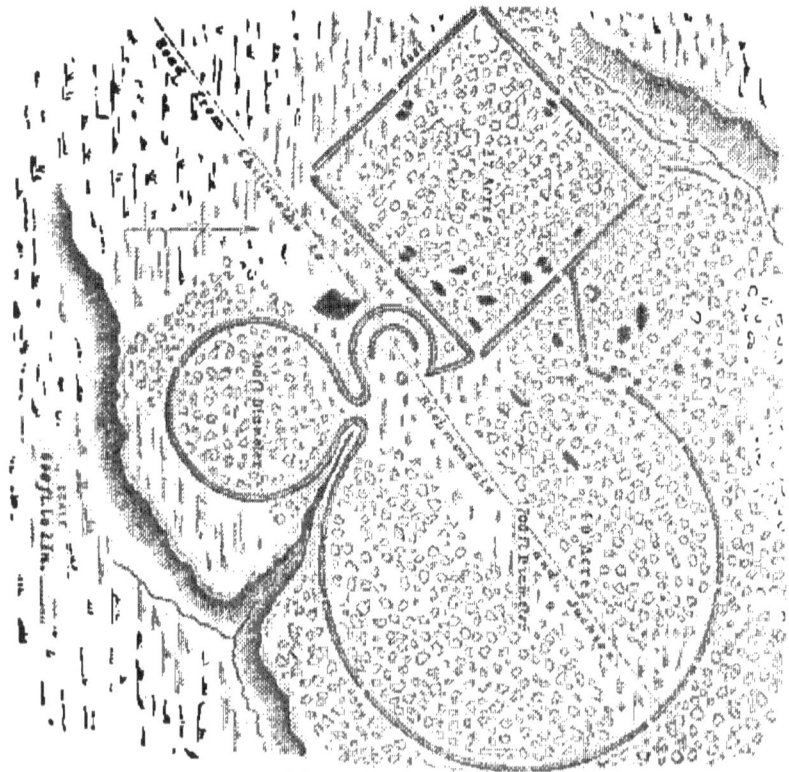

Fig. 15.—Works near Liberty, Ohio.

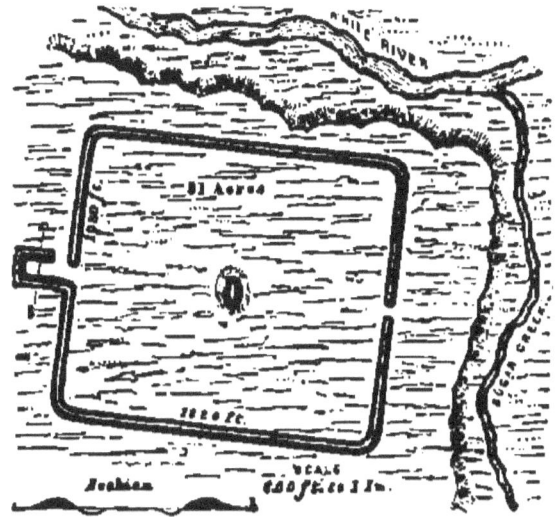

Fig. 16.—Rectangular Work, Randolph County, Indiana.

important works of the Mound-Builders, chiefly in Ohio. Relics of art have been dug from some of the mounds, consisting of a considerable variety of ornaments and implements, made of copper, silver, obsidian, porphyry, and greenstone, finely wrought. There are axes, single and double; adzes, chisels, drills or gravers, lance-heads, knives, bracelets, pendants, beads, and the like, made of copper. There are articles of pottery, elegantly designed and finished; ornaments made of silver, bone, mica from the Alleghanies, and shells from the Gulf of Mexico.

The articles made of stone show fine workmanship; some of them are elaborately carved. Tools of some very hard material must have been required to work the porphyry in this manner. Obsidian is a volcanic product largely used by the ancient Mexicans and Peruvians for arms and cutting instruments. It is found in its natural state nowhere nearer the Mississippi Valley than the Mexican mountains of Cerro Gordo.

There appears to be evidence that the Mound-Builders had the art of spinning and weaving, for cloth has been found among their remains. At the meeting of the International Congress of Pre-Historic Archæology held at Norwich, England, in 1868, one of the speakers stated this fact as follows: "Fragments of charred cloth made of spun fibres have been found in the mounds. A specimen of such cloth, taken from a mound in Butler County, Ohio, is in Blackmore Museum, Salisbury. In the same collection are several lumps of burnt clay which formed part of the 'altar,' so called, in a mound in Ross County, Ohio: to this clay a few charred threads are still attached." Figures 17 and 18 represent specimens of vases taken from the mounds.

Figs. 17, 18.—Vases from the Mounds.

Mr. Schoolcraft gives this account of a discovery made in West Virginia: "*Antique tube: telescopic device.* In the course of excavations made in 1842 in the easternmost of the three mounds of the Elizabethtown group, several tubes of stone were disclosed, the precise object of which has been the subject of various opinions. The longest measured twelve inches, the shortest eight. Three of them were carved out of steatite, being skillfully cut and polished. The diameter of the tube externally was one inch and four tenths; the bore, eight tenths of an inch. This calibre was continued till within three eighths of an inch of the sight end, when it diminishes to two tenths of an inch. By placing the eye at the diminished end, the extraneous light is shut from the pupil, and distant objects are more clearly discerned."

He points out that the carving and workmanship generally are very superior to Indian pipe carvings, and adds, if this article was a work of the Mound-Builders "intended for a telescopic tube, it is a most interesting relic." An ancient Peruvian relic, found a few years since, shows the figure of a man wrought in silver, in the act of studying the heavens through such a tube. Similar tubes have been found among relics of the Mound-Builders in Ohio and elsewhere. In Mexico, Captain Dupaix saw sculptured on a peculiar stone structure the figure of a man making use of one. Astronomical devices were sculptured below the figure. This structure he supposed to have been used for observation of the stars. His account of it will be given in the chapter on Mexican and Central American ruins.

The Mound-Builders used large quantities of copper such as that taken from the copper beds on Lake Superior, where the extensive mines yield copper, not in the ore, but as pure metal. It exists in those beds in immense masses, in small veins, and in separated lumps of various sizes. The Mound-Builders worked this copper without smelting it. Spots of pure silver are frequently found studding the surface of Lake Superior copper, and appearing as if welded to it, but not alloyed with it. No other copper has this peculiarity; but copper with similar blotches of silver has been dug from the mounds. It was naturally inferred from this fact that the ancient people represented by these antiquities had some knowledge of the art of mining copper which had been used in the copper region of Lake Superior. This inference finally became an ascertained fact.

THEIR ANCIENT MINING WORKS.

Remains of their mining works were first discovered in 1848 by Mr. S. O. Knapp, agent of the Minnesota Mining Company, and in 1849 they were described by Dr. Charles T. Jackson, in his geological report to the national government. Those described were found at the Minnesota mine, in upper Michigan, near Lake Superior. Their mining was chiefly surface work; that is to say, they worked the surface of the veins in open pits and trenches. At the Minnesota mine, the greatest depth of their excavations was thirty feet; and here, "not far below the bottom of a trough-like cavity, among a mass of leaves, sticks, and water, Mr. Knapp discovered a detached mass of copper weighing nearly six tons. It lay upon a cob-work of round logs or skids six or eight inches in diameter, the ends of which showed plainly the marks of a small axe or cutting tool about two and a half inches wide. They soon shriveled and decayed when exposed to the air. The mass of copper had been raised several feet, along the foot of the lode, on timbers, by means of wedges." At this place was found a stone maul weighing thirty-six pounds, and also a copper maul or sledge weighing twenty-five pounds. Old trees showing 395 rings of annual growth stood in the débris, and "the fallen and decayed trunks of trees of a former generation were seen lying across the pits." Figure 19 (opposite) presents a section of this mining shaft of the Mound-Builders: *a* shows the mass of copper; *b* the bottom of the shaft; *c* the earth and débris which had been thrown out. The dark spots are masses of copper.

The modern mining works are mostly confined to that part of the copper region known as Keweenaw Point. This is a projection of land extending into Lake Superior, and described as having the shape of an immense horn. It is about eighty miles in length, and, at the place where it joins the main land, about forty-five miles in width. All through this district, wherever modern miners have worked, remains of ancient mining works are abundant; and they are extensive on the adjacent island, known as Isle Royale. The area covered by the ancient works is larger than that which includes the modern mines, for they are known to exist in the dense forests of other districts, to which the modern mining has not yet been extended.

One remarkable mining excavation of the Mound-Builders was found near the Waterbury mine. Here, in the face of a vertical bluff, was discovered "an ancient, artificial, cavern-like recess, twenty-five feet in horizon-

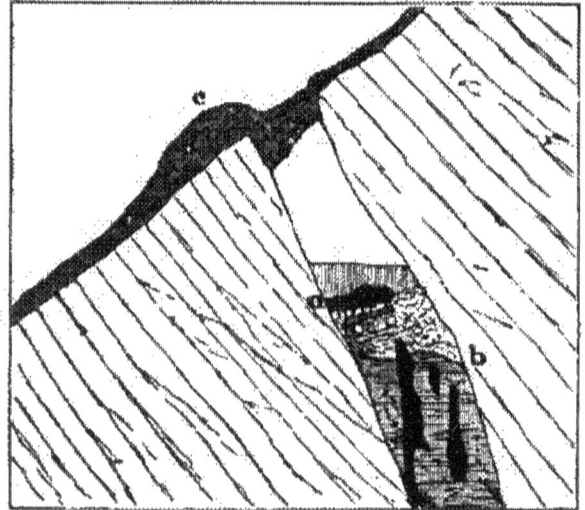

Fig. 19.—Ancient Mining Shaft.

tal length, fifteen feet high, and twelve feet deep. In front of it is a pile of excavated rock on which are standing, in full size, the forest trees common to this region." Some of the blocks of stone removed from this recess would weigh two or three tons, and must have required levers to get them out. Beneath the surface rubbish were the remains of a gutter or trough made of cedar, placed there to carry off water from the mine. At the bottom of the excavation a piece of white cedar timber was found on which were the marks of an axe. Cedar shovels, mauls, copper gads or wedges, charcoal, and ashes were discovered, over which "primeval" forest trees had grown to full size.

Modern mining on Lake Superior began effectively in 1845. The whole copper region has not been fully explored. Works of the ancient miners are found at all the mines of any importance; and they show remarkable skill in discovering and tracing actual veins of the metal. Colonel Charles Whittlesey, one of the best authorities on this point, believes the Mound-Builders worked the copper-beds of that region during "a great length of time," and more of their works will undoubtedly be explored when the forests shall be cleared away from those portions of the copper region not yet worked by modern miners. So far as they have been traced, they every where show the same methods, the same implements, and the same peculiarities of both knowledge and lack of knowledge in the old miners.

II.

ANTIQUITY OF THE MOUND-BUILDERS.

THAT the Mound-Builders and their works belong to a distant period in the past is evident; but, of course, we have no means of determining their antiquity with any approach to accuracy, no scheme of chronology by which their distance from us in time can be measured. Nevertheless, some things observed in their remains make it certain that the works are very ancient.

1. One fact showing this is pointed out by those who have examined them carefully as follows: None of these works (mounds and inclosures) occur on the lowest-formed of the river terraces, which mark the subsidence of the western streams; and as there is no good reason why their builders should have avoided erecting them on that terrace, while they raised them promiscuously on all the others, it follows, not unreasonably, that this terrace has been formed since the works were erected. It is apparent, also, that in some cases the works were long ago partly destroyed by streams which have since receded more than half a mile, and at present could not reach them under any circumstances. Those streams generally show four successive terraces, which mark four distinct eras of their subsidence since they began to flow in their present courses. The fourth terrace, on which none of

the works are found, marks the last and longest of these periods; and it marks also the time since the Mound-Builders ceased to occupy the river-valleys where it was formed. The period marked by this fourth terrace must be the longest, because the excavating power of such streams necessarily diminishes as their channels grow deeper. This geological change, which has taken place since the latest of the mounds and inclosures were constructed, shows that the works are very old; no one can tell how old. To count the years is impossible; but we can see that the date, if found, would take us back to a remote period in the past.

2. Great antiquity is indicated by the skeletons taken from the mounds. Every skeleton of a Mound-Builder is found in a condition of extreme decay. It sometimes appears that the surface of a mound has been used by the wild Indians for interments; but their skeletons, which are always found well preserved, can be readily distinguished by their position in the mounds, as well as by other peculiarities. The decayed bones of Mound-Builders are invariably found within the mounds, never on the surface, usually at the bottom of the structure, and nearly always "in such a state of decay as to render all attempts to restore the skull, or, indeed, any part of the skeleton, entirely hopeless." Not more than one or two skeletons of that people have been recovered in a condition suitable for intelligent examination. It is stated in the work of Squier and Davis that the only skull belonging incontestably to an individual of the Mound-Building race, which has been preserved entire,

was taken from a mound situated on a knoll (itself artificial apparently) on the summit of a hill, in the Scioto Valley, four miles below Chillicothe.

What, save time itself, can have brought these skeletons to a condition in which they fall to pieces when touched, and are ready to dissolve and become dust? All the circumstances attending their burial were unusually favorable for their preservation. The earth around them has invariably been found "wonderfully compact and dry." And yet, when exhumed, they are in such a decomposed and crumbling condition that to restore them is impossible. Sound and well-preserved skeletons, known to be nearly two thousand years old, have been taken from burial-places in England, and other European countries less favorable for preserving them. The condition of an ancient skeleton can not be used as an accurate measure of time, but it is sufficiently accurate to show the difference between the ancient and the modern, and in this case it allows us to assume that these extremely decayed skeletons of the Mound-Builders are much more than two thousand years old.

Those familiar with the facts established by geologists and palæontologists are aware that remains of human skeletons have been discovered in deposits of the "Age of Stone" in Western Europe; not to any great extent, it is true, although the discoveries are sufficient to show that fragments of skeletons belonging to that age still exist. It is not without reason, therefore, that the condition of decay in which all skeletons of the Mound-Builders are exhumed from their burial-places is considered a proof of their great antiquity. There is no other explanation which, so far as appears, can be reasonably accepted.

3. The great age of these mounds and inclosures is shown by their relation to the primeval forests in which most of them were discovered. I say *primeval* forests, because they seemed primeval to the first white men who explored them. Of course there were no unbroken forests at such points as the Ohio Valley, for instance, while they were occupied by the Mound-Builders, who were a settled agricultural people, whose civilized industry is attested by their remains. If they found forests in the valleys they occupied, these were cleared away to make room for their towns, inclosures, mounds, and cultivated fields; and when, after many ages of such occupation, they finally left, or were driven away, a long period must have elapsed before the trees began to grow freely in and around their abandoned works. Moreover, observation shows that the trees which first make their appearance in such deserted places are not regular forest trees. The beginning of such growths as will cover them with great forests comes later, when other preliminary growths have appeared and gone to decay.

When the Ohio Valley was first visited by Europeans it was covered by an unbroken forest, most of the trees being of great age and size; and it was manifest that several generations of great forest trees had preceded those found standing in the soil. The mounds and inclosures were discovered in this forest, with great trees growing in them. Eight hundred rings of annual growth

Antiquity of the Mound-Builders. 51

were counted in the trunk of a tree mentioned by Sir Charles Lyell and others, which was found growing on a mound at Marietta. In the same way, successive generations of forest trees had grown over their extensive mining works near Lake Superior, and many of those works are still hidden in what seem to be primeval forests.

General Harrison made the following suggestion in regard to the establishment of those forests in Ohio. When the individual trees that first got possession of the soil had died out one after another, they would, in many cases, be succeeded by other kinds, till at last, after a great number of centuries, that remarkable diversity of species characteristic of North America would be established. His suggestion, the result of practical observation and study, is not without reason. It is certain, in any case, that the period when these old constructions were deserted is so far back in the past, that sufficient time has since passed for the abandoned towns and fields to remain for years, and perhaps centuries, as waste places, pass through the transition from waste lands to the beginning of forest growths, and then be covered by several generations of such great forest trees as were cleared away to prepare the soil for the settlements, towns, and farms of our people.

HOW LONG WERE THEY HERE?

There are many indications to warrant the conclusion that the Mound-Builders occupied their principal seats in the Ohio and Mississippi Valleys during a very long period. If they came from the south, as appears evident, their settlements must have been extended up the valley gradually. After their first communities were established in the Gulf regions, considerable time must have elapsed before their advancing settlements were extended northward, through the intervening region, into the Valley of the Ohio. On the Ohio and in the valleys of its tributaries their settlements were very numerous, and evidently populous. The surprising abundance of their works in this region, which have been traced in our time, shows that they dwelt here in great numbers, and had no lack of industry.

This region seems to have been one of the principal centres from which their settlements were advanced into the western part of Virginia; into Michigan, Wisconsin, Iowa, Illinois, Indiana, and Missouri. The spread of their settlements was necessarily gradual, and a long period must have been required to extend them over all the country where remains of their works are known to exist. If their civilization was chiefly developed after their arrival in the country, which is unlikely, many years must have elapsed before colonies went forth, to any great extent, from the original seat of its development. In any case, time was required to make their chief settlements sufficiently old and populous to send forth colonies. It is manifest in their remains that the communities of this ancient people most remote from the populous centres on the Ohio, east, north, and west, were, like all border settlements, the rudest and least populous. The remains at these points do not indicate either as much wealth or as many workers, and the places where these borderers settled must have been the latest occupied and the earliest abandoned. One diligent investigator, who believes they came originally from Mexico, speaks of the time of their stay in the country as follows:

"When we consider the time required to people the whole extent of the territory where their remains are found, and bring that people into a condition to construct such monuments, and when we reflect on the interval that must have passed after their construction until the epoch of their abandonment, we are constrained to accord them a very high antiquity."

He points out that they were sun worshipers, like the Mexicans and Peruvians, and calls attention to the disks dug from their mounds, which appear to have been designed as representations of the sun and moon.

Their long occupation of the country is suggested by the great extent of their mining works. All who have examined these works agree with Colonel Whittlesey that they worked the Lake Superior copper mines "for a great length of time." How long they had dwelt in the Ohio Valley when this mining began can not be told, but a very considerable period must have elapsed after their arrival at that point before the mines were discovered. We can not suppose the first settlers who came up from the Gulf region to the Ohio Valley went on immediately, through the wilderness a thousand miles, to hunt for copper mines on Lake Superior; and, even after they began to explore that region, some time must have passed before the copper was found.

After they discovered the mines and began to work them, their progress could not have been rapid. As their open trenches and pits could be worked only in the summers, and by methods that made their operations much slower than those of modern miners, no great advance of their work was possible during the working time of each season; and yet remains of their mining works have been discovered wherever mines have been opened in our day; and, as previously stated, they are known to exist in heavy forests, where the modern mining works have not yet been established. There is nothing to indicate that they had settlements any where in the mining region. Colonel Whittlesey, and others whose study of the subject gives their opinion much weight, believe the Mound-Builders went up from the settlements farther south in the summers, remained in the copper region through the season, and worked the mines in organized companies until the advance of winter terminated their operations.

Colonel Whittlesey says: "As yet, no remains of cities, graves, domiciles, or highways have been found in the copper region;" and adds, "as the race appears to have been farther advanced in civilization than their successors, whom we call aborigines, they probably had better means of transportation than bark canoes." It may be said, also, that the accumulations called wealth were necessary to make this regular and systematic mining possible. Without these they could not have provided the supplies of every kind required to sustain organized companies of miners through a single season. A great many summers must have passed away before such companies of miners, with all needed tools and supplies, could have made their works so extensive by means of such methods as they were able to use.

They probably occupied the country on the Gulf and Lower Mississippi much longer than any other portion of the great valley. Their oldest and latest abandoned settlements appear to have been in this region, where, we may reasonably suppose, they continued to dwell long after they were driven from the Ohio Valley and other places at the north.

The Natchez Indians found settled on the Lower Mississippi may have been a degenerate remnant of the Mound-Builders. They differed in language, customs, and condition from all other Indians in the country; and their own traditions connected them with Mexico. Like the Mexicans, they had temples or sacred buildings in which the "perpetual fire" was maintained. Each of their villages was furnished with a sacred building of this kind. They had also peculiarities of social and political organization different from those of other tribes. They were sun-worshipers, and claimed that their chief derived his descent from the sun. The Natchez were more settled and civilized than the other Indians, and, in most respects, seemed like another race. One learned investigator classes them with the Nahuatl or Toltec race, thinks they came from Mexico, and finds that, like the ancient people of Panuco and Colhuacan, they had the phallic ceremonies among their religious observances. Their history can not be given, and there is little or nothing but conjecture to connect them with the Mound-Builders. The Natchez were exterminated in 1730 by the French, whom they had treated with great kindness. Of the few who escaped death, some were received among the Chickasaws and Muskogees, but more were sent to Santo Domingo and sold as slaves.

No view that can be taken of the relics left by the Mound-Builders will permit us to believe their stay in the country was short. Any hypothesis based on the shortest possible estimate of the time must count the years by centuries.

III.

WHO WERE THE MOUND-BUILDERS?

This ancient people, whose remains indicate unity and civilization, must have been organized as a nation, with a central administration which all recognized. They must have had a national name, but nobody can tell certainly what it was. No record or tradition has preserved it, unless discovery of it can be made in a national designation found, without clear explanation, in the old books and traditions of Central America, and applied to some country situated at a distance from that part of the continent in the northeast. These old books and traditions mention "Huehue-Tlapalan" as a distant northeastern country, from which the Nahuas or Toltecs came to Mexico; and Brasseur de Bourbourg, who has translated one of the old books and given much attention to others, supposes the Toltecs and the Mound-Builders to be the same people, or did suppose this previous to the appearance of his "Atlantic theory." But this point will be more fully considered when we come to the Central American antiquities.

Some antiquaries suggest that the Mound-Builders were the people called "Allighewi" in old traditions of the Iroquois, but we have nothing to make this very probable. The Iroquois were somewhat superior to the other great family of barbarous Indians in organization for the business of fighting. There are some reasons for believing they came to the lake regions and the Ohio Valley much earlier than the Algonquin branch of the wild Indian race. It is permissible, at least, to conjecture, if one feels inclined to do so, that it was the Iroquois migration from the northwest, or that of the great family to which the Iroquois family belonged, which expelled the Mound-Builders from their border settlements, cut them off from the copper mines, and finally pushed them down the Mississippi; but nothing more than conjecture is possible in this case, and the supposition gives the Iroquois migration a greater antiquity than may be allowable. Moreover, the traditionary lore of the wild Indians had nothing to say of the Mound-Builders, who appear to have been as unknown and mysterious to these Indians as they are to us.

NOT ANCESTORS OF THE WILD INDIANS.

Some inquirers, not always without hesitation, suggest that the Indians inhabiting the United States two hundred years ago were degenerate descendants of the Mound-Builders. The history of the world shows that civilized communities may lose their enlightenment, and sink to a condition of barbarism; but the degraded descendants of a civilized people usually retain traditional recollections of their ancestors, or some traces of the lost civilization, perceptible in their customs and their legendary lore. The barbarism of the wild Indians of North America had nothing of this kind. It was original barbarism. There was nothing to indicate that either the Indians inhabiting our part of the continent, or their ancestors near or remote, had ever been civilized, even to the extent of becoming capable of settled life and organized industry. And, besides, the constant tradition of these Indians, supported by concurring circumstantial evidence, appears to warrant the belief that they came to this part of the continent originally from the west or northwest, at a period too late to connect them in this way with the Mound-Builders.

Two hundred years ago the Valley of the Mississippi, and the regions east of it, were occupied by two great families of Indians, the Iroquois and the Algonquins, each divided into separate tribes. Between these two families there was a radical difference of language. The Indians of New England were Algonquins. The Iroquois dwelt chiefly in New York, and around Lake Erie, from Niagara to Detroit, although separate communities of the group to which they immediately belonged were found in other places, such as the Dacotahs and Winnebagoes at the West, and the isolated Tuscaroras of the Carolinas. Mr. Lewis H. Morgan, who has discussed "Indian Migrations" in several interesting papers printed in the North American Review, thinks the Iroquois were separated very early from the same original stem which produced the great Dacotah family. The Algonquins were spread most widely over the country when it was first visited by Europeans.

Among all these Indians there was a tradition that their ancestors came from a distant region in the Northwest, and this tradition is accepted as true by those who have studied them most carefully. Mr. Morgan supposes they came across the continent, and estimates that not less than a thousand years must have passed between the departure of the various groups of the Algonquin family from a common centre in the northwest and the condition in which they were found two hundred years ago. When Europeans began to explore North America, this family had become divided into several branches, and each of these branches had a modified form of the common language, which, in turn, had developed several dialects. A long period was required to effect so great a change; but, whatever estimate of the time may be accepted, it seems to be a fact that the Algonquins came to the Mississippi Valley long after the Mound-Builders left it, and also later than the Iroquois or Dacotah family. That the Iroquois preceded the Algonquins at the East appears to be indicated by the relative position of the two families in this part of the country. Mr. Parkman, in his work on "The Jesuits in North America," describes it as follows: "Like a great island in the midst of the Algonquins lay the country of tribes speaking the generic tongue of the Iroquois."

There is no trace or probability of any direct relationship whatever between the Mound-Builders and the barbarous Indians found in the country. The wild Indians of this continent had never known such a condition as that of the Mound-Builders. They had nothing in common with it. In Africa, Asia, and elsewhere among the more uncultivated families of the human race, there is not as much really *original* barbarism as some anthropologists are inclined to assume; but there can be no serious doubt that the wild Indians of North America were original barbarians, born of a stock which had never, at any time, been either civilized or closely associated with the influences of civilization.

Some of the pottery and wrought ornaments of the Mound-Builders is equal in finish and beauty to the finest manufactured by the ancient Peruvians. They constructed artificial ponds like the aguadas in Central America. They used sun-dried brick, especially at the South, where walls of this material have been discovered supporting some of the mounds and embankments. They manufactured cloth. But their intelligence, skill, and civilized ways are shown not only by their constructions and manufactures, but also by their mining works. Who can imagine the Iroquois or the Algonquins working the copper mines with such intelligence and skill, and such a combination of systematic and persistent industry! They had no tradition of such a condition of life, no trace of it. It is absurd to suppose a relationship, or a connection of any kind, between the original barbarism of these Indians and the civilization of the Mound-Builders. The two peoples were entirely distinct and separate from each other. If they really belonged to the same race, which is extremely doubtful, we must go back through unnumbered ages to find their common origin and the date of their separation.

BRERETON'S STORY.

Those who seek to identify the Mound-Builders with the barbarous Indians find nothing that will support their hypothesis. Nevertheless, some of them have tried very strangely to give it aid by one or two quotations from early voyagers to America. The most important are taken from Brereton's account of Gosnold's voyage in 1602. The following occurred on the coast of Maine:

"Eight Indians, in a Basque shallop, with mast and sail, an iron grapple, and a kettle, came boldly aboard us, one of them appareled with a waistcoat and breeches of black serge, made after our sea fashion, hose and shoes on his feet: all the rest (saving one that had a pair of breeches of blue cloth) were naked."

It is known that the Basques were accustomed to send fishing vessels to the northeastern coast of America long before this continent was discovered by Columbus. They continued to do this after the discovery. These Indians had evidently become well acquainted with the Basques, and, therefore, did not fear to approach Gosnold's ship. Probably some of them had been employed on board Basque fishing vessels. Certainly their boat and apparel came from the Basque fishermen, and did not show them to be Mound-Builders. Of the Indians on the coast of Massachusetts, Brereton says:

"They had great store of copper, some very red, some of a paler color; none of them but have chains, earrings, or collars of this metal. They had some of their arrows herewith, much like our broad arrow-heads, very workmanly made. Their chains are many hollow pieces cemented together, each piece of the bigness of one of our reeds, a finger in length, ten or twelve of them together on a string, which they wear about their necks: their collars they wear about their bodies like bandeliers a handful broad, all hollow pieces like the other, but somewhat shorter, four hundred pieces in a collar, very fine and evenly set together." He adds: "I am persuaded they have great store (of flax) growing upon the main, as also mines and many other rich commodities, which we, wanting time, could not possibly discover."

If all this had been true, it would not serve the purpose for which it is quoted; for remains of the Mound-Builders have never existed in Massachusetts, and we should necessarily suppose these Indians had procured copper and copper ornaments by trading with the Basques or with other French voyagers. If only one or two Indians had been represented as wearing ornaments made of copper, this explanation could be readily accepted. But he avers that they had "great store of copper," and adds, "None of them but have chains, earrings, or collars of this metal." Therefore his statement is incredible. The following considerations will show why it must not be regarded as honest, unadorned truth.

1. Those interested in Gosnold's voyage aimed to establish a colony on that coast; and all who served them, or were controlled by them, were easily moved to tell seductive stories of the country "upon the main." The chief aim of Brereton's account of this voyage was to incite emigration. Therefore he gave this wonderfully

colored account of mines, flax-growing, copper chains
and collars, and "other rich commodities" among the
wild Indians of Massachusetts. Settlements on that
coast, it was believed, would bring profit to those in
whose interest he wrote. Gosnold actually proposed at
that time to establish a colony on one of the islands in
Buzzard's Bay, and had with him twenty men who were
expected to stay as colonists, but finally refused to do
so. He saw a great deal of the Indians, and knew much
more of their actual condition than the story admits.

2. Eighteen years later the Pilgrims landed at Plymouth from the Mayflower. Neither copper mines nor
flax fields were then known in Massachusetts. No Indians with "great store" of copper and flax, and covered
with copper ornaments, were seen or heard of by the
Pilgrims, either at that time or afterward. In 1602,
Brereton, or any other writer employed to write in such
a way as would promote emigration, could tell such stories, and romance freely concerning the Indians, without
fear of contradiction. Afterward, when the actual barbarism of the Indian tribes in New England and other
parts of the country had become generally known, no
one could describe any of these Indians as successful
miners and flax-growers, and assert gravely that they
had such stores of copper that "none of them" lacked
great abundance of copper "chains, earrings, collars,"
and the like, without being laughed at. Brereton's story
must be regarded as an invention designed to serve a
special purpose, but not warranted by any thing seen
during the voyage he describes. Neither in New En-

gland nor any where else in our part of the continent did the early colonists find Indians who worked copper mines and had "great store of copper." What Brereton says was not true of any Indians known to our first colonists or to their successors. It corresponds to no reality found in any part of our territory during the last two hundred and fifty years. Therefore, to use his story in support of an absurd hypothesis is not a satisfactory proceeding.

AMERICAN ETHNOLOGY.

It may be true that all the aboriginal peoples found inhabiting North and South America, save the Esquimaux, belonged originally to the same race. Some writers assume it to be true, although it seems strongly improbable, not to say impossible. If they were all of the same race, time and development, under different conditions of life, had divided this race into at least two extremely unlike branches. The wild Indians of North America were profoundly different from the ancient people of Central America and Peru. The Pueblo or Village Indians of New Mexico have scarcely any thing in common with the Apaches, Comanches, and Sioux. Even the uncivilized Indians of South America are different from those in the United States. Our wild Indians have more resemblance to the nomadic Koraks and Chookchees found in Eastern Siberia, throughout the region that extends to Behring's Strait, than to any people on this continent. Those who have seen these Siberians, traveled with them, and lived in their tents, have found the resemblance very striking; but I infer from what they say that the Korak or Chookchee is superior to the Indian. See Kennan's "Tent Life in Siberia."

Mr. Lewis H. Morgan finds evidence that the American aborigines had a common origin in what he calls "their systems of consanguinity and affinity." If it can be made to appear beyond question that these systems prevail and are identical every where from Patagonia to the Arctic Zone, his argument will have great force. But this has not yet been shown. He says: "The Indian nations, from the Atlantic to the Rocky Mountains, and from the Arctic Sea to the Gulf of Mexico, with the exception of the Esquimaux, have the same system. It is elaborate and complicated in its general form and details; and, while deviations from uniformity occur in the systems of different stocks, the radical features are, in the main, constant. This identity in the essential characteristics of a system so remarkable tends to show that it must have been transmitted with the blood to each stock from a common original source. It affords the strongest evidence yet obtained of unity in origin of the Indian nations within the region defined."

But unity in race among wild Indians found within the region specified would be sufficiently manifest without this evidence. That the same system of consanguinity and affinity, with precisely the same features of identity, ever was extended over the whole continent, remains unproved. The supposed traces of it among the Pueblos are by no means clear. A more complete and accurate research is required to show that identically the same system ever has existed any where between the United States and Patagonia. A system not wholly unlike it, though not the same, might grow up any where in widely separated tribal communities of barbarous peoples, without doing any thing more than the tribal system itself to show a common origin in race.

The aborigines of America may have been originally all of the same race. There are some considerations in favor of this hypothesis which have been used by writers entitled to great respect; but it can not yet be claimed with reason that they have been able to settle this question beyond the reach of doubt, even in their own minds. Therefore, to speak moderately, it would be premature to assume that the Mound-Builders were even remotely of the same race with the wild Indians, from whom they were so different in all we know of them.

The attempt to establish this hypothesis of identity in race has given rise to a tendency to underrate the development of the ancient people of Mexico and Central America, and to lower the estimate of their attainments sufficiently to bring them within reach of close relationship to the wild Indians. The difficulty being reduced in this way, there follows an attempt to get rid of it entirely, and establish connection between these unlike peoples, by talking of "Semi-Village Indians." But the hypothesis used in this case is not well warranted by facts. Such "Semi-Village Indians" as are supposed, really standing half way between the savages and the Pueblos, and being actually savages half developed into Pueblos, have never had a clearly defined and unquestionable existence here since the continent became known to Europeans. In the border region between the northern wild Indians and the old Mexican race there are exceptional communities formed by association or mixture, but we can not reasonably give them the significance claimed for the supposed "Semi-Village Indians." Moreover, these exceptional communities are usually Pueblos whose habits have been changed and their civilization lessened by association with wild Indians, or in some other way. The Navajos began their present condition by fleeing to the mountains from the Spaniards. The Mound-Builders, who must have been, still more than the Pueblos, unlike the barbarous Indians, can not be explained by any reference whatever to such communities. If they were of the same race, they were far from being the same people.

Some ethnologists, whose suggestions are entitled to respectful attention whether accepted or rejected, specify considerations which they believe forbid us to regard the ancient Mexicans and the northern wild Indians as identical in race. They point to the well known fact that the fauna of the American continent below the northern frontier of Mexico is remarkably different from that between this line and the Arctic Sea. At the north, America abounds in species similar to those of Europe and Asia, with some admixture of forms wholly American, while at the south the old-world forms disappear, and the fauna of the whole region between Mexico and Cape Horn becomes "as peculiar as that of Australia."

The explanation given is, that during the glacial period

the larger part of North America, like Northern Asia and Europe, was covered with ice and partly submerged, and that the fauna found in this part of North America was introduced after the glacial period by immigration from Asia and Europe over connecting lands or islands at the northwest and the northeast, and perhaps by some migration from the south; the fauna at the south meanwhile remaining very much as it was before, with very little change through later migrations from the north.

Professor Huxley called attention to this subject in a brief address to the London Ethnological Society in 1869. After stating the case, he presented the following queries and suggestions: "The Austro-Columbian fauna, as a whole, therefore, existed antecedently to the glacial epoch. Did man form part of that fauna? To this profoundly interesting question no positive answer can be given; but the discovery of human remains associated with extinct animals in the caves of Brazil, by Lund, lends some color to the supposition. Assuming this supposition to be correct, we should have to look in the human population of America, as in the fauna generally, for an indigenous or Austro-Columbian element, and an immigrant or 'Arctogeal' element." He then suggests that the Esquimaux may now represent the immigrant element, and the old Mexican and South American race that which was indigenous, and that the "Red Indians of North America" may have appeared originally as a mixture of these two races. He adds, very reasonably, "It is easy to suggest such problems as these, but quite impossible, in the present state of our knowledge, to solve them."

WHO WERE THE MOUND-BUILDERS?

They were unquestionably American aborigines, and not immigrants from another continent. That appears to me the most reasonable suggestion which assumes that the Mound-Builders came originally from Mexico and Central America. It explains many facts connected with their remains. In the Great Valley their most populous settlements were at the south. Coming from Mexico and Central America, they would begin their settlements on the Gulf coast, and afterward advance gradually up the river to the Ohio Valley. It seems evident that they came by this route; and their remains show that their only connection with the coast was at the south. Their settlements did not reach the coast at any other point.

Their constructions were similar in design and arrangement to those found in Mexico and Central America. Like the Mexicans and Central Americans, they had many of the smaller structures known as *teocallis*, and also large high mounds, with level summits, reached by great flights of steps. Pyramidal platforms or foundations for important edifices appear in both regions, and are very much alike. In Central America important edifices were built of hewn stone, and can still be examined in their ruins. The Mound-Builders, like some of the ancient people of Mexico and Yucatan, used wood, sun-dried brick, or some other material that could not resist decay. There is evidence that they used timber for building purposes. In one of the mounds opened in the Ohio Valley two chambers were found with remains of the timber of which the walls were made, and with arched ceilings precisely like those in Central America, even to the overlapping stones. Chambers have been found in some of the Central American and Mexican mounds, but there hewn stones were used for the walls. In both regions the elevated and terraced foundations remain, and can be compared. I have already called attention to the close resemblance between them, but the fact is so important in any endeavor to explain the Mound-Builders that I must bring it to view here.

Consider, then, that elevated and terraced foundations for important buildings are peculiar to the ancient Mexicans and Central Americans; that this method of construction, which, with them, was the rule, is found nowhere else, save that terraced elevations, carefully constructed, and precisely like theirs in form and appearance, occupy a chief place among the remaining works of the Mound-Builders. The use made of these foundations at Palenque, Uxmal, and Chichen-Itza, shows the purpose for which they were constructed in the Mississippi Valley. The resemblance is not due to chance. The explanation appears to me very manifest. This method of construction was brought to the Mississippi Valley from Mexico and Central America, the ancient inhabitants of that region and the Mound-Builders being the same people in race, and also in civilization, when it was brought here.

A very large proportion of the old structures in Ohio and farther south called "mounds," namely, those which are low in proportion to their horizontal extent, are terraced foundations for buildings, and if they were situated in Yucatan, Guatemala, and Southern Mexico, they would never be mistaken for any thing else. The high mounds also in the two regions are remarkably alike. In both cases they are pyramidal in shape, and have level summits of considerable extent, which were reached by means of stairways on the outside. The great mound at Chichen-Itza is 75 feet high, and has on its summit a ruined stone edifice; that at Uxmal is 60 feet high, and has a similar ruin on its summit; that at Mayapan is 60 feet high; the edifice placed on its summit has disappeared. The great mound at Miamisburg, Ohio, is 68 feet high; and that at Grave Creek, West Virginia, is 75 feet high. Both had level summits, and stairways on the outside, but no trace of any structure remains on them. All these mounds were constructed for religious uses, and they are, in their way, as much alike as any five Gothic churches.

Could these works of the Mound-Builders be restored to the condition in which they were when the country was filled with their busy communities, we should doubtless see great edifices, similar in style to those in Yucatan, standing on the upper terraces of all the low and extended "mounds," and smaller structures on the high mounds, such as those above named. There would seem to be an extension of ancient Mexico and Central America through Texas into the Mississippi and Ohio valleys; and so, if there were no massive stone-work in the old ruins of those countries, it might seem that the Mound-

Builders' works were anciently extended into them by way of Texas.

The fact that the settlements and works of the Mound-Builders extended through Texas and across the Rio Grande indicates very plainly their connection with the people of Mexico, and goes far to explain their origin. We have other evidence of intercourse between the two peoples; for the obsidian dug from the mounds, and perhaps the porphyry also, can be explained only by supposing commercial relations between them.

We can not suppose the Mound-Builders to have come from any other part of North America, for nowhere else north of the Isthmus was there any other people capable of producing such works as they left in the places where they dwelt. Beyond the relics of the Mound-Builders themselves, no traces of the former existence of such a people have been discovered in any part of North America save Mexico, and Central America, and districts immediately connected with them. At the same time, it is not unreasonable to suppose the civilized people of these regions extended their settlements through Texas, and also migrated across the Gulf into the Mississippi Valley. In fact, the connection of settlements by way of Texas appears to have been unbroken from Ohio to Mexico.

This colonizing extension of the old Mexican race must have taken place at a remote period in the past; for what has been said of the antiquity of the Mound-Builders shows that a very long period, far more than two thousand years, it may be, must have elapsed since they left the Valley of the Ohio. Perhaps they found

D

the country mostly unoccupied, and saw there but little of any other people until an irruption of warlike barbarians came upon them from the Northwest.

In speculating on the causes of their withdrawal after centuries of occupation, absolute certainty is impossible, and we have no means of going much beyond mere conjecture. We may suppose as most probable that an influx of barbarians destroyed their border settlements, interrupted their mining operations, and caused them to retire gradually toward the Gulf. Fragments of their communities may have become incorporated with the barbarous tribes. This conjecture has been used to explain certain exceptional peculiarities noticed in some of the wild Indian tribes. For instance, it has been suggested that the Mandan Indians were a separated and lost fragment of the mound-building people, they being noticeably unlike other Indians in many respects, lighter in color, and peculiar in manners and customs. What is conjectured may be true, but we have no means of proving its truth. That the Mandans were like what a lost community of Mound-Builders might have become by degeneration through mixture and association with barbarians may be supposed, but the actual history of that remarkable tribe might give its peculiarities a very different explanation. The Mandans were supposed to be a branch of the Dacotahs. They may have been, like the Navajos, a changed community of Pueblos, but any attempt to explain them by means of conjecture is useless.

The supposition that the Toltecs and the Mound-Builders were the same people seems to me not improbable. The reasons for it will be stated when we come to a discussion of the antiquities, books, and traditions of Central America. I will only say here that, according to dates given in the Central American books, the Toltecs came from "Huehue-Tlapalan," a distant country in the northeast, long previous to the Christian era. They played a great part and had a long career in Mexico previous to the rise of their successors in power, the Aztecs, who were overthrown by the Spaniards.

IV.

MEXICO AND CENTRAL AMERICA.

Ruins and other vestiges revealing an ancient civilization are found throughout the whole southern section of North America, extending as far north as New Mexico and Arizona. But here the antiquities do not all belong to the same period in the past, nor exhibit unvarying likeness and unity of civilized life. They are somewhat less homogeneous, and do not constantly represent the same degree of civilization. In this region, the monuments suggest successive and varying periods in the civilized condition of the old inhabitants, some of the oldest and most mysterious monuments seeming to indicate the highest development.

In the northern part of this region we find ruins of great buildings similar in plan and arrangement to those still used by the Pueblos, but far superior as monuments of architecture, science, and skill, and much more unlike those farther south than is apparent in the principal structures of the Mound-Builders. They show that the old settlers in the Mississippi Valley did not belong to the Pueblo branch of the Mexican race. Farther south, in the central part of the region specified, development was more advanced. Here, in the last ages of American ancient history, was the seat of the Mexican or Aztec civilization, but the monuments in this part of the country are mostly older than the Aztec period. The most astonishing remains are found still farther south, in Chiapa, Tabasco, Oxaca, Yucatan, Honduras, Tehuantepec, Guatemala, and other parts of Central America. In this southern region, mostly buried in heavy forests, are wonderful ruins of great cities and temples. Only a small part of modern Mexico is included in the region where these ruins are situated, and most of them, probably, were not much better understood by the ancient Mexicans than they are by us. Many of those explored in later times were unknown to that people, just as others, more in number, doubtless, than those already described, still remain unvisited and unknown in the great and almost impenetrable forests of the country.

THE NORTHERN REMAINS.

The ruins in Northern Mexico, including New Mexico and Arizona, consist chiefly, as already stated, of the remains of structures similar in general design and purpose to those of the Village Indians, the Pueblos. In the more ancient times, doubtless, as at present, a large proportion of the dwellings and other edifices, like those in the Mississippi Valley, were built of perishable materials which have left no trace. Many of them, however, were built of stone, and have left ruins which show their character. Stone ruins are common in this northern region, although wood and adobe seems to have been more commonly used as building material. Some of the ruined stone edifices were inhabited when the country was conquered by the Spaniards. The remains present every where the same characteristics. They represent a people who built always in the same way, with some variations in the forms of their structures, and had substantially the same condition of life; but the ruins are not all of the same age. Their character can be sufficiently shown by describing a few of them.

In New Mexico, west of the Rio Grande, between the head waters of the San Jose and Zuni rivers, a bluff or ridge rises in a valley two hundred feet high. The Spaniards named it "El Moro." One side of this bluff is vertical, and shows yellowish-white sandstone rock, on the face of which are inscriptions; "Spanish inscriptions and Indian hieroglyphics." It was carefully described in 1849 by Lieutenant Simpson, and was explored again four or five years later by Lieutenant A. W. Whipple, who described it in his report to the government, published in the third volume of " Explorations and Surveys for a Railroad Route to the Pacific." On the summit of this height, which Lieutenant Simpson named " Inscription Rock," are the ruins of an extensive Pueblo edifice built of stone. The walls were built "with considerable skill." In some places they are still " perfect to the height of six or eight feet, vertical, straight, and smooth; and the masonry is well executed, the stones being of uniform size—about fourteen inches long and six wide." The layers are horizontal, each successive layer breaking joints with that below it. Remains of cedar beams were discovered, and also obsidian arrow-heads, painted pottery, and other relics. Another ruin was seen on a height across the gorge. It was found to be similar to this, both in character and condition of decay.

Lieutenant Whipple went westward along the thirty-fifth parallel. We can not do better than follow the report of what he saw.

His next stopping-place, after leaving "El Moro," was in the beautiful valley of Ojo Pescado. Here, close by a spring that showed artificial stone-work of ancient date, were two old Pueblo buildings in ruins, "so ancient that the traditions of present races do not reach them." Not far away is a deserted town of later date. The two ancient structures were circular in form and equal in size, each being about eight hundred feet in circumference. They were built of stone, but the walls have crumbled and become chiefly heaps of rubbish. The pottery found here, like that at "El Moro," is "painted with bright

Fig. xi.—Pueblo Hulu at Pecos.

colors, in checks, bands, and wavy stripes; many fragments show a beautiful polish. A few pieces were discovered larger in size, inferior in color and quality, but indicating a more fanciful taste. United, they formed an urn with a curious handle; a frog painted on the outside and a butterfly within." In the same neighborhood, on the summit of a cliff twenty feet high, was another old ruin "strongly walled around." In the centre was a mound on which were traces of a circular edifice.

The next place of encampment was at Zuni, where, as shown in Figure 21, can be seen one of these great Pueblo buildings inhabited by two thousand people (Lieutenant Whipple's estimate). It has five stories, the walls of each receding from those below it. Looking from the top, he says it reminded him of a busy ant-hill, turkeys and tamed eagles constituting a portion of its inhabitants. Not more than a league away is an "old Zuni" which shows nothing but ruins. Its crumbling walls, worn away until they are only from two to twelve feet high, are "crowded together in confused heaps over several acres of ground." This old town became a ruin in ancient times. After remaining long in a ruined condition it was again rebuilt, and again deserted after a considerable period of occupation. It is still easy to distinguish the differences in construction between the two periods. "The standing walls rest upon ruins of greater antiquity;" and while the primitive masonry is about six feet thick, that of the later period is only from a foot to a foot and a half thick. Small blocks of sandstone were used for the latter. Heaps of débris cover a considerable

Fig. 21.—Modern Zuni.

space, in which, among other things, are relics of pottery and of ornaments made of sea-shells. Pieces of quaintly-carved cedar posts were found here, and their condition of decay, compared with that of the cedar beams at "El Moro," "indicated great antiquity." The place of this ruin is now one of the consecrated places of the Village Indians; it has "a Zuni altar" which is constantly used and greatly venerated. On leaving the place, their guide blew a white powder toward the altar three times, and muttered a prayer. This, he explained, was "asking a blessing of Montezuma and the sun." This altar seems to represent recollections of the ancient sun-worship.

At a place west of Zuni ancient relics were found, indicating that an extensive Pueblo town had formerly stood there, but "the structures were probably of adobes," as there was no débris of stone walls, and only very faint traces of foundations. Near the Colorado Chiquito is an extensive ruin, on the summit of an isolated hill of sandstone, the faces of its walls being here and there visible above heaps of débris. It appears to be very old. As near as could be ascertained, the great rectangular Pueblo building was three hundred and sixty feet in extent on one side, and one hundred and twenty on the other. In some places the walls are ten feet thick, "with small rooms inserted in them." Stone axes, painted pottery, and other articles are found in the débris: "The indented pottery, said to be so very ancient, is found here in many patterns." On a ridge overlooking the valley of Pueblo Creek are traces of an old settlement of large extent, supposed to have been that heard of in 1539 by the friar Marco de Niça as "the kingdom of Totonteac." Adobe seems to have been used here for building. Traces of other ruins were seen in various places, and springs along the route showing ancient stone-work are mentioned.

Ruins are abundant in the Rio Verde Valley down to the confluence of that river with the Rio Salinas. It is manifest that this whole region was anciently far more populous than it is now. Lieutenant Whipple says, "Large fields in the valley of the Rio Gila, and many spots among the Pinal Lena Mountains, are marked with the foundations of adobe houses." Figure 22 represents a Pueblo ruin in the Valley of the Gila. "In Cañon

Fig. 22.—Pueblo Ruins in the Valley of the Gila.

Chelly, near San Francisco Mountain, and upon Rio Verde, there are ruins of more permanent structures of stone, which in their day must have excelled the famed Pueblos of New Mexico." There was a higher degree of civilization in the ancient times, so far as relates to architecture and skill in the arts and appliances of life, than has been shown by people of the same race dwelling there in our time; but the ancient condition of life seems to have been maintained from age to age without material change.

THE "SEVEN CITIES OF CEVOLA."

In the New Mexican valley of the Chaco, one degree or more north of Zuni, are ruins of what some suppose to have been the famous "Seven Cities of Cevola." In 1540, Spanish cupidity having been strongly incited by tales of the greatness and vast wealth of Cevola, Coronado, then governor of New Galicia, set out with an army to conquer and rob its cities. The report in which he tells the story of this conquest and of his disappointment is still in existence. The Cevolans defended themselves with arrows and spears, and hurled stones upon his army from the tops of their buildings. But resistance was of no avail; Cevola was conquered by Coronado, and immediately deserted by all its inhabitants who escaped death. The conquering buccaneer, however, did not find the treasures of gold and silver he expected. Three hundred and thirty years or more have passed away since this expedition of the Spanish marauders was undertaken, but the "Seven Cities of Cevola" (if they really were the "cities" whose remains are found in the Chaco Valley), although much dilapidated, are still sufficiently well preserved to show us what they were.

There are seven ruins in the Chaco Valley, all of the same age, from one to three miles apart, the whole line along which they are situated being not more than ten miles in extent. Coronado said of Cevola, "The seven cities are seven small towns, standing all within four leagues together;" and "all together they are called Cevola." The Chaco ruins show that each of those "cities" was, Pueblo fashion, a single edifice of vast size, capable of accommodating from five hundred to three thousand people. They were all built of stone, around three sides of a square, the side opposite the main building being left open. Figure 23 represents one of these buildings restored, according to Lieutenant Simpson. Figure 24 is a ground plan of this structure. The outer faces of the walls were constructed with thin and regular blocks of sandstone; the inner surfaces were made of cobblestone laid in mortar, and the outer walls were three feet thick. They were four or five stories high, and the only entrances to them were "window openings" in the second story. Above the cañon inclosing the valley containing these ruins, at a distance of thirteen miles, are the remains of another "city" of precisely the same kind. Its walls are at present between twenty and thirty feet high, their foundations being deeply sunk into the earth. Lieutenant Simpson, who explored that region in 1849, says it was built of tabular pieces of hard, fine-grained, compact gray sandstone, none of the layers being more

Fig. 24.—Pueblo Building, restored.

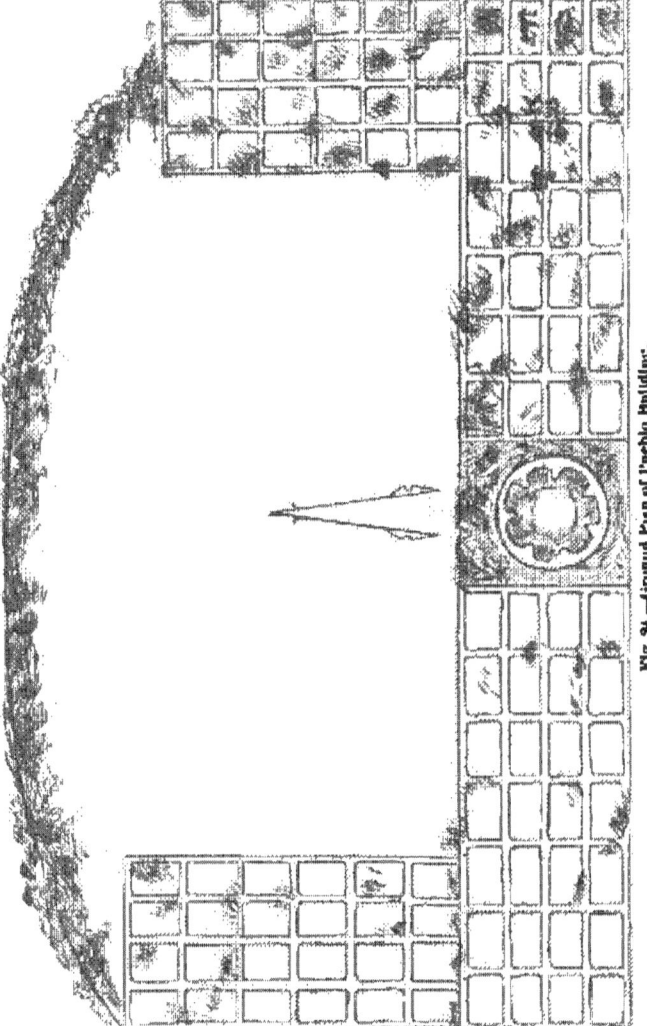

Fig. 34.—Ground Plan of Pueblo Building.

than three inches thick. He adds, "It discovers in the masonry a combination of science and art which can only be referred to a higher stage of civilization and refinement than is discoverable in the work of Mexicans or Pueblos of the present day. Indeed, so beautifully diminutive and true are the details of the structure as to cause it at a little distance to have all the appearance of a magnificent piece of mosaic."

Other ruins have been examined in this northern part of the old Mexican territory, and more will be brought to light, for the whole region has not been carefully examined, and new discoveries are constantly reported.

CENTRAL MEXICO.

As we go down into Central Mexico, the remains assume another character, and become more important; but the antiquities in this part of the country have not been very completely explored and described, the attention of explorers having been drawn more to the south. Some of them are well known, and it can be seen that to a large extent they are much older than the time of the Aztecs whom Cortez found in power.

In the northern part of the Mexican Valley was the city of Tulha, the ancient capital of the Toltecs. At the time of the conquest its site was an extensive field of ruins. At Xochicalco, in the State of Mexico, is a remarkable pyramid, with a still more remarkable base. It was constructed with five stages or stories, and stands on a hill consisting chiefly of rock, which was excavated and hollowed for the construction of galleries and chambers. The opening serves as an entrance to several galleries, which are six feet high and paved with cement, their sides and ceilings seeming to have been covered with some very durable preparation which made them smooth and glistening. Captain Dupaix found the main gallery sixty yards, or one hundred and eighty feet long, terminating at two chambers which are separated only by two massive square pillars carefully fashioned of portions of the rock left for the purpose by the excavators. Over a part of the inner chamber, toward one corner, is a dome or cupola six feet in diameter at the base, and rather more in height. It has a regular slope, and was faced with square stones well prepared and admirably laid in cement. From the top went up a tube or circular aperture nine inches in diameter, which probably reached the open air or some point in the pyramid.

In this part of Mexico can be seen, among other things, the great pyramid or mound of Cholulu, the very ancient and remarkable pyramidal structures at Teotihuacan, and an uncounted number of *teocallis* or pyramids of smaller size. The pyramid of Cholulu covers an area of forty-five acres. It was terraced and built with four stages. When measured by Humboldt it was 1400 feet square at the base, and 160 feet high. At present it is a ruin, and, to superficial observers, seems little more than a huge artificial mound of earth. Its condition of decay indicates that it is much older than even the Toltec period. The largest structure at Teotihuacan covers eleven acres. These structures, and the Mexican *teocallis* generally, were made of earth, and faced with brick or stone.

Captain Dupaix saw, not far from Antequera, two
truncated pyramids which were penetrated by two carefully constructed galleries. A gallery lined with hewn
stone, bearing sculptured decorations, went through one
of them. A similar gallery went partly through the
other, and two branches were extended at right angles
still farther, but terminating within. He mentions also
the ruins of elaborately decorated edifices which had
stood on elevated terraces. At one place he excavated
a terraced mound, and discovered burnt brick; and he
describes two ancient bridges of the Tlascalans, both
built of hewn stone laid in cement, one of them being
200 feet long and 36 wide. Obelisks or pillars 42 feet
high stood at the corners of these bridges. Important
remains of the ancient people exist in many other places;
and "thousands of other monuments unrecorded by the
antiquaries invest every sierra and valley of Mexico with
profound interest."

At Papantla, in the State of Vera Cruz, there is a
very ancient pyramidal structure somewhat peculiar in
style and character. It is known that important ruins
exist in the forests of Papantla and Mesantla which
have never been described. The remarkable pyramid
at Papantla was examined and described by Humboldt.
The only material employed in constructing it was hewn
stone. The stone was prepared in immense blocks,
which were laid in mortar. The pyramid was an exact
square at the base, each side being 82 feet in length, and
the height about 60 feet. The stones were admirably
cut and polished, and the structure was remarkably sym-

metrical. Six stages could be discerned by Humboldt, and his account of it says, "A seventh appears to be concealed by the vegetation which covers the sides of the pyramid." A great flight of steps leads to the level summit, by the sides of which are smaller flights. "The facing of the stones is decorated with hieroglyphics, in which serpents and crocodiles carved in relievo are visible. Each story contains a great number of square niches symmetrically distributed. In the first story there are 24 on each side, in the second 20, and in the third 16. There are 366 of these niches on the whole pyramid, and 12 in the stairs toward the east."

The civilization of the Aztecs who built the old city of Mexico will be made a separate topic; but it may be said here that when they came into the Valley of Mexico they were much less advanced in civilization than their predecessors. There is no reason whatever to doubt that they had always resided in the country as an obscure branch of the aboriginal people. Some have assumed, without much warrant, that they came to Mexico from the North. Mr. Squier shows, with much probability, that they came from the southern part of the country, where communities are still found speaking the Aztec language. When they rose to supremacy they adopted, so far as their condition allowed, the superior knowledge of their predecessors, and continued, in a certain way, and with a lower standard, the civilization of the Toltecs. It has been said, not without reason, that the civilization found in Mexico by the Spanish conquerors consisted, to a large extent, of "fragments from the wreck that befell the American civilization of antiquity."

THE GREAT RUINS AT THE SOUTH.

To find the chief seats and most abundant remains of the most remarkable civilization of this old American race, we must go still farther south into Central America and some of the more southern states of Mexico. Here ruins of many ancient cities have been discovered, cities which must have been deserted and left to decay in ages previous to the beginning of the Aztec supremacy. Most of these ruins were found buried in dense forests, where, at the time of the Spanish Conquest, they had been long hidden from observation.

The ruins known as Palenque, for instance, seem to have been entirely unknown to both natives and Spaniards until about the year 1750. Cortez and some of his companions went through the open region near the forest in which these ruins are situated without hearing of them or suspecting their existence. The great ruins known as Copan were in like manner unknown in the time of Cortez. The Spaniards assaulted and captured a native town not far from the forest that covered them, but heard nothing of the ruins. The captured town, called Copan, afterward gave its name to the remains of this nameless ancient city, which were first discovered in 1576, and described by the Spanish licentiate Palacios. This was little more than forty years after the native town was captured; but, although Palacios tried, "in all possible ways," to get from the older and more intelligent natives some account of the origin and history of the ruined city, they could tell him nothing about it.

To them the ruins were entirely mythical and mysterious. With the facts so accessible, and the antiquity of the ruins so manifest, it is very singular that Mr. Stephens fell into the mistake of confounding this ruined city, situated in an old forest that was almost impenetrable, with the town captured by the Spaniards. The ruins here were discovered accidentally; and to approach them it was necessary, as at Palenque, to cut paths through the dense tropical undergrowth of the forest.

To understand the situation of most of the old ruins in Central America, one must know something of the wild condition of the country. Mr. Squier says:

"By far the greater proportion of the country is in its primeval state, and covered with dense, tangled, and almost impenetrable tropical forests, rendering fruitless all attempts at systematic investigation. There are vast tracts untrodden by human feet, or traversed only by Indians who have a superstitious reverence for the moss-covered and crumbling monuments hidden in the depths of the wilderness. * * * For these and other reasons, it will be long before the treasures of the past, in Central America, can become fully known."

A great forest of this character covers the southern half of Yucatan, and extends far into Guatemala, which is half covered by it. It extends also into Chiapa and Tabasco, and reaches into Honduras. The ruins known as Copan and Palenque are in this forest, not far from its southern edge. Its vast depths have never been much explored. There are ruins in it which none but wandering natives have ever seen, and some, perhaps, which no human foot has approached for ages. It is believed that ruins exist in nearly every part of this vast wilderness.

According to the old Central American books and traditions, some of the principal seats of the earliest civilization, that of the "Colhuas," was in this forest-covered region. In their time the whole was cultivated and filled with inhabitants. Here was a populous and important part of the Colhuan kingdom of "Xibalba," which, after a long existence, was broken up by the Toltecs, and which had a relation, in time, to the Aztec dominion of Montezuma, much like that of the old monarchy of Egypt to the kingdom of the Ptolemies.

In the time of the Spaniards there was in the forest at Lake Peten a solitary native town, founded nearly a century previous to their time by a Maya prince of Itza, who, with a portion of his people, fled from Yucatan to that lonely region to escape from the disorder and bloodshed of a civil war. This was the civil war which destroyed Mayapan, and broke up the Maya kingdom of Yucatan. In 1695, Don Martin Ursua, a Spanish official, built a road from Yucatan to Lake Peten, captured the town, and destroyed it. He reported that the builders of this road found evidence that "wrecks of ancient cities lie buried in this wilderness." All along the route they discovered vestiges of ruins, and special mention is made of "remains of edifices on raised terraces, deserted and overgrown, and apparently very ancient."

CHARACTER OF THE SOUTHERN RUINS.

Should you visit the ruins of one of these mysterious old cities, you would see scattered over a large area great edifices in different stages of decay, which were erected on the level summits of low pyramidal mounds or platforms. The summits of these mounds are usually of sufficient extent to furnish space for extensive terraces or "grounds," as well as room for the buildings. The edifices were built of hewn stone laid in a mortar of lime and sand, the masonry being admirable, and the ornamentation, in most cases, very abundant. The pyramid-foundations of earth were faced with hewn stone, and provided with great stone stairways. These, we may suppose, were the most important buildings in the old city. The ordinary dwellings, and all the other less important structures, must have been made chiefly of wood or some other material, which had perished entirely long ago and left no trace, for at present their remains are no more visible than those of the forest leaves which grew five hundred years ago.

One explorer of Palenque says: "For five days did I wander up and down among these crumbling monuments of a city which, I hazard little in saying, must have been one of the largest ever seen." There is, however, nothing to show us certainly the actual size of any of these ancient cities. It is manifest that some of them were very large; but, as only the great structures made of stone remain to be examined, the actual extent of the areas covered by the other buildings can not be determined.

Fig. 23.—Arch of Las Monjas.

The chief peculiarity of these ruins, that which especially invites attention, is the evidence they furnish that their builders had remarkable skill in architecture and architectural ornamentation. All who have visited them bear witness that the workmanship was of a high order. The rooms and corridors in these edifices were finely and often elaborately finished, plaster, stucco, and sculpture being used. In one room of a great building at Uxmal Mr. Stephens says "the walls were coated with a very fine plaster of Paris, equal to the best seen on walls in this country." Speaking of the construction of this edifice, he says, "throughout, the laying and polishing of the stones are as perfect as under the rules of the best modern masonry." All the ruins explored have masonry of the same character. The floors, especially of the courts and corridors, were made sometimes of flat stones admirably wrought and finely polished, and sometimes of cement, which is now "as hard as stone." Mr. Stephens, describing corridors of the "Palace" at Palenque, says "the floors are of cement, as hard as the best seen in the remains of Roman baths and cisterns." We give two illustrations of their method of constructing the arch. Figure 25 shows an arch of Las Monjas, at Uxmal. Figure 26 shows the most common form of the arch in the older ruins.

The ornamentation is no less remarkable than the masonry and architectural finish. It is found on the walls within and without, and appears in elaborate designs on the heavy cornices. The exterior ornamentation is generally carved or sculptured on the smooth sur-

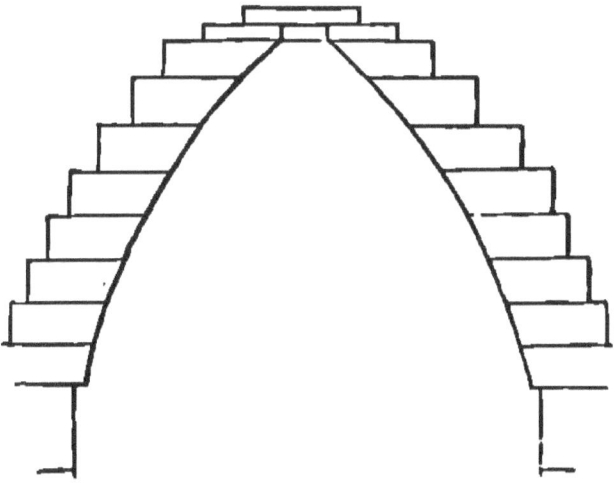

Fig. 26.—Common Form of Arch.

face of the stone, and must have required a vast amount of time and labor, as well as skillful artists. In some of the ruins inscriptions are abundant, being found on walls, tablets, and pillars. The general effect of the exterior decoration is thus described by Mr. Stephens in the account of his first view of the ruins at Palenque: "We saw before us a large building richly ornamented with stuccoed figures on pilasters, curious and elegant; trees growing close to it, and their branches entering the doors; the style and effect of structure and ornament unique, extraordinary, and mournfully beautiful." In a description of the walls around an interior court of a building at Uxmal, we have this tribute to the artistic skill of the decorators: "It would be difficult, in arranging four sides facing a court-yard, to have more variety, and, at the same time, more harmony of ornament."

In some of the ruins, and especially at Copan, there are clusters of four-sided stone pillars or obelisks varying from twelve to over twenty feet high. These are elaborately sculptured, and show human figures, ornamental designs, and many inscriptions. One or two statues have been discovered, and a statuette twelve inches high is described; "it is made of baked clay, very hard, and the surface is smooth as if coated with enamel." At Palenque are remains of a well-built aqueduct; and near the ruins, especially in Yucatan, are frequently found the remains of many finely constructed aguadas or artificial lakes. The bottoms of these lakes were made of flat stones laid in cement, several layers deep. In Yucatan traces of a very ancient paved road have been found. This road ran north and south, and probably led to cities in the region now covered by the great wilderness. It was raised above the graded level of the ground, and made very smooth.

These antiquities show that this section of the continent was anciently occupied by a people admirably skilled in the arts of masonry, building, and architectural decoration. Some of their works can not be excelled by the best of our constructors and decorators. They were highly skilled, also, in the appliances of civilized life, and they had the art of writing, a fact placed beyond dispute by their many inscriptions.

A more particular account of some of these ruins will

be given in the next chapter. Among the more important works relating to them are those of Stephens and Catherwood, some of the volumes of Mr. Squier, Frederick Waldeck's work, and a recent French volume by Desiré Charnay, which is accompanied by a folio volume of photographs. Palacios, who described Copan in 1576, may properly be called the first explorer. A brief account of Palenque was prepared by Captain Del Rio in 1787, and published in 1822. Captain Dupaix's folios, in French, with the drawings of Castañada, contain the first really important memoir on these ruins. It was prepared in 1807, detained in Mexico during the Mexican Revolution, and finally published at Paris in 1834–5. The volumes of Brasseur de Bourbourg are valuable. They relate chiefly to matters not always understood, and seldom discussed with care, by those who merely visit and describe the monuments, such as the writing, books, and traditions of the ancient Mexican and Central American people. His style is diffuse, sometimes confused, and rather tedious; and some of his theories are very fanciful. But he has discovered the key to the Maya alphabet and translated one of the old Central American books. No careful student of American archæology can afford to neglect what he has written on this subject.

V.

MEXICO AND CENTRAL AMERICA.

To understand the situation and historical significance of the more important antiquities in Southern Mexico and Central America, we must keep in view their situation relative to the great unexplored forest to which attention has been called. Examine carefully any good map of Mexico and Central America, and consider well that the ruins already explored or visited are wholly in the northern half of Yucatan, or far away from this region, at the south, beyond the great wilderness, or in the southern edge of it. Uxmal, Mayapan, Chichen-Itza, and many others, are in Yucatan. Palenque, Copan, and others are in the southern part of the wilderness, in Chiapa, Honduras, and Guatemala. Mr. Squier visited ruins much farther south, in San Salvador, and in the western parts of Nicaragua and Costa Rica.

The vast forest which is spread over the northern half of Guatemala and the southern half of Yucatan, and extended into other states, covers an area considerably larger in extent than Ohio or Pennsylvania. Does its position relative to the known ruins afford no suggestion concerning the ancient history of this forest-covered region? It is manifest that, in the remote ages when the older of the cities now in ruins were built, this region

' was a populous and important part of the country. And
this is shown also by the antiquities found wherever it
has been penetrated by explorers who knew how to make
discoveries, as well as by the old books and traditions.
Therefore it is not unreasonable to assume that Copan
and Palenque are specimens of great ruins that lie buried
in it. The ruins of which something is known have
merely been visited and described in part by explorers,
some of whom brought away drawings of the principal
objects. In giving a brief account of the more important ruins, I will begin with the old city of which most
has been heard.

PALENQUE.

No one can tell the true name of the ancient city now
called Palenque. It is known to us by this name because the ruins are situated a few miles distant from the
town of Palenque, now a village, but formerly a place of
some importance. The ruins are in the northern part
of the Mexican State of Chiapa, hidden out of sight in
the forest, where they seem to have been forgotten long
before the time of Cortez. More than two hundred years
passed after the arrival of the Spaniards before their existence became known to Europeans. They were discovered about the year 1750. Since that year decay has
made some progress in them. Captain Del Rio, who visited and described them in 1787, examined "fourteen edifices" admirably built of hewn stone, and estimated the
extent of the ruins to be "seven or eight leagues one
way [along the River Chacamas], and half a league the

other." He mentions "a subterranean aqueduct of great solidity and durability, which passes under the largest building."

Other explorers have since visited Palenque, and reported on the ruins by pen and pencil; but it is not certain that all the ruined edifices belonging to them have been seen, nor that the explorations have made it possible to determine the ancient extent of the city with any approach to accuracy. The very great difficulties which obstruct all attempts at complete exploration have not allowed any explorer to say he has examined or discovered all the mouldering monuments hidden in the dense and tangled forest, even within the space allowed by Del Rio's "half league" from the river, not to speak of what may lie buried and unknown in the dense mass of trees and undergrowth beyond this limit.

The largest known building at Palenque is called the "Palace." It stands near the river, on a terraced pyramidal foundation 40 feet high and 310 feet long, by 260 broad at the base. The edifice itself is 228 feet long, 180 wide, and 25 feet high. It faces the east, and has 14 doorways on each side, with 11 at the ends. It was built entirely of hewn stone, laid with admirable precision in mortar which seems to have been of the best quality. A corridor 9 feet wide, and roofed by a pointed arch, went round the building on the outside; and this was separated from another within of equal width. The "Palace" has four interior courts, the largest being 70 by 80 feet in extent. These are surrounded by corridors, and the architectural work facing them is richly decorated. Within the building were many rooms. From the north side of one of the smaller courts rises a high tower, or pagoda-like structure, thirty feet square at the base, which goes up far above the highest elevation of the building, and seems to have been still higher when the whole structure was in perfect condition. The great rectangular mound used for the foundation was cased with hewn stone, the workmanship here, and every where else throughout the structure, being very superior. The piers around the courts are "covered with figures in stucco, or plaster, which, where broken, reveals six or more coats or layers, each revealing traces of painting." This indicates that the building had been used so long before it was deserted that the plastering needed to be many times renewed. There is some evidence that painting was used as a means of decoration; but that which most engages attention is the artistic management of the stone-work, and, above all, the beautifully executed sculptures for ornamentation.

Two other buildings at Palenque, marked by Mr. Stephens, in his plan of the ruins, as "Casa No. 1" and "Casa No. 2," views of which are shown in Figures 27 and 28, are smaller, but in some respects still more remarkable. The first of these, 75 feet long by 25 wide, stands on the summit of a high truncated pyramid, and has solid walls on all sides save the north, where there are five doorways. Within are a corridor and three rooms. Between the doorways leading from the corridor to these rooms are great tablets, each 13 feet long and 8 feet high, and all covered with elegantly-carved

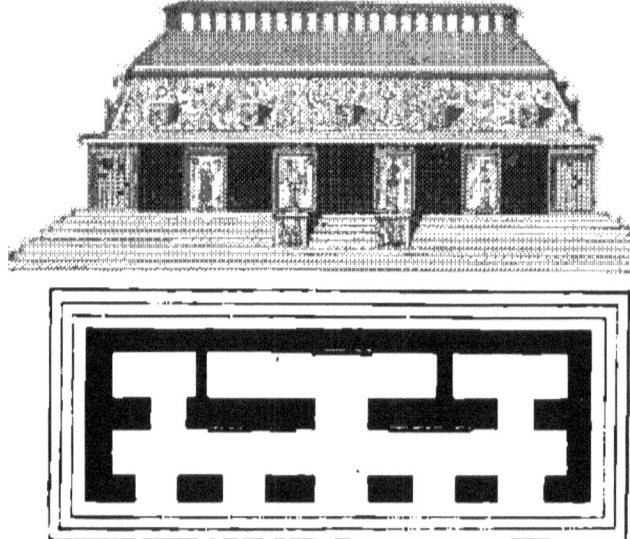

Fig. 77.—Casa No. 1, Palenque—Front View and Ground Plan.

inscriptions. A similar but smaller tablet, covered with an inscription, appears on the wall of the central room.

"Casa No. 2" consists of a steep and lofty truncated pyramid, which stands on a terraced foundation, and has its level summit crowned with a building 50 feet long by 31 wide, which has three doorways at the south, and within a corridor and three rooms. This edifice, sometimes called "La Cruz," has, above the height required for the rooms, what is described as "two stories of interlaced stucco-work, resembling a high, fanciful lattice." Here, too, inscribed tablets appear on the walls; but the inscriptions, which are abundant at Palenque, are by no

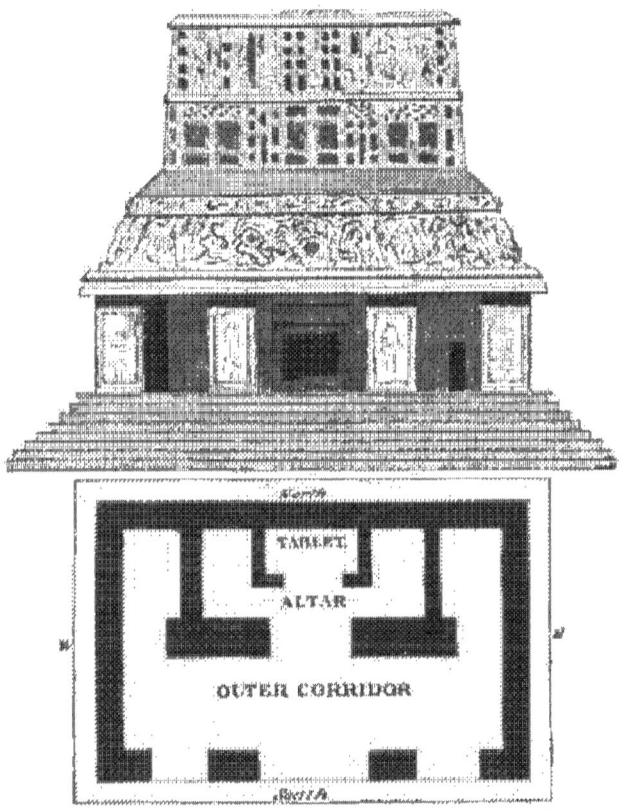

Fig. 23.—Casa No. 2, Palenque (La Cruz)—Front View and Ground Plan.

means confined to tablets. As to the ornamentation, the walls, piers, and cornices are covered with it. Every where the masterly workmanship and artistic skill of the old constructors compel admiration; Mr. Stephens going so far as to say of sculptured human figures found in fragments, "In justness of proportion and symmetry they must have approached the Greek models."

"Casa No. 2" of Mr. Stephens is usually called "La Cruz" because the most prominent object within the building is a great bas-relief on which are sculptured a cross and several human figures. This building stands on the high pyramid, and is approached by a flight of steps. Dupaix says, "It is impossible to describe adequately the interior decorations of this sumptuous temple." The cross is supposed to have been the central object of interest. It was wonderfully sculptured and decorated; human figures stand near it, and some grave ceremony seems to be represented. The infant held toward the cross by one of the figures suggests a christening ceremony. The cross is one of the most common emblems present in all the ruins. This led the Catholic missionaries to assume that knowledge of Christianity had been brought to that part of America long before their arrival; and they adopted the belief that the Gospel was preached there by St. Thomas. This furnished excellent material for the hagiologists of that age; but, like every thing else peculiar to these monkish romancers, it betrayed great lack of knowledge.

The cross, even the so-called Latin cross, is not exclusively a Christian emblem. It was used in the Oriental world many centuries (perhaps millenniums) before the Christian era. It was a religious emblem of the Phœnicians, associated with Astarte, who is usually figured bearing what is called a Latin cross. She is seen so

figured on Phœnician coin. The cross is found in the
ruins of Nineveh. Mr. Layard, describing one of the
finest specimens of Assyrian sculpture (the figure of "an
early Nimrod king" he calls it), says: "Round his neck
are hung the four sacred signs; the crescent, the star or
sun, the trident, and *the cross*." These "signs," the cross
included, appear suspended from the necks or collars of
Oriental prisoners figured on Egyptian monuments known
to be fifteen hundred years older than the Christian era.
The cross was a common emblem in ancient Egypt, and
the Latin form of it was used in the religious mysteries
of that country, in connection with a monogram of the
moon. It was to degrade this religious emblem of the
Phœnicians that Alexander ordered the execution of two
thousand principal citizens of Tyre by crucifixion.

The cross, as an emblem, is very common among the
antiquities of Western Europe, where archæological investigation has sometimes been embarrassed and confused by the assumption that any old monument bearing
the figure of a cross can not be as old as Christianity.

What more will be found at Palenque, when the
whole field of its ruins has been explored, can not now
be reported. The chief difficulty by which explorers
are embarrassed is manifest in this statement of Mr.
Stephens: "Without a guide, we might have gone within a hundred feet of the buildings without discovering
one of them." More has been discovered there than I
have mentioned, my purpose being to give an accurate
view of the style, finish, decoration, and general character of the architecture and artistic work found in the

ruins rather than a complete account of every thing connected with them. The ruins of Palenque are deemed important by archæologists partly on account of the great abundance of inscriptions found there, which, it is believed, will at length be deciphered, the written characters being similar to those of the Mayas, which are now understood.

COPAN AND QUIRIGUA.

The ruins known as Copan are situated in the extreme western part of Honduras, where they are densely covered by the forest. As already stated, they were first discovered by Europeans about forty years after the war of the conquest swept through that part of the country, and were at that time wholly mysterious to the natives. The monuments seem older than those at Palenque, but we have only scant descriptions of them. They are situated in a wild and solitary part of the country, where the natives "see as little of strangers as the Arabs about Mount Sinai, and are more suspicious." For this reason they have not been very carefully explored. It is known that these ruins extend two or three miles along the left bank of the River Copan. Not much has been done to discover how far they extend from the river into the forest.

Mr. Stephens describes as follows his first view of them: "We came to the right bank of the river, and saw directly opposite a stone wall from 60 to 90 feet high, with furze growing out of the top, running north and south along the river 624 feet, in some places fallen, in others entire." This great wall supported the rear side of the elevated foundation of a great edifice. It was made of cut stone well laid in mortar or cement, the blocks of stone being 6 feet long. Figure 29 shows the wall somewhat imperfectly. He saw next a square

Fig. 29.—Great Wall at Copan.

stone column standing by itself, 14 feet high and 3 feet on each side. From top to bottom it was richly ornamented with sculptured designs on two opposite sides, the other sides being covered with inscriptions finely carved on the stone. On the front face, surrounded by the sculptured ornaments, was the figure of a man. Fourteen other obelisks of the same kind were seen, some of them being higher than this. Some of them had fallen. These sculptured and inscribed pillars constitute the chief peculiarity of Copan. Mr. Squier says of them: "The ruins of Copan, and the corresponding monuments which I examined in the valley of the Chamelican, are distinguished by singular and elaborately carved *monoliths*, which seem to have been replaced at Palenque by equally elaborate *basso relievos*, belonging, it would seem, to a later and more advanced period of art."

The great building first noticed stands, or stood, on a pyramidal foundation, which is supported along the river by that high back wall. The structure extends 624 feet on the river line. Mr. Stephens described it as an "oblong inclosure," and states that it has a wide terrace nearly 100 feet above the river, on which great trees are growing, some of them more than 20 feet in circumference. Here, as at Palenque, the ornamentation was "rich and abundant." The ruins, greatly worn by decay, still show that "architecture, sculpture, painting, and all the arts that embellish life had flourished in this overgrown forest." Some beautifully executed sculptures were found buried in the earth, and there can be no doubt that extensive excavation, if it were possible in that almost invincible forest, would lead to important and valuable discoveries. Besides the great building and the monoliths, several pyramidal structures are mentioned by Mr. Stephens, who points out that extensive exploration is impossible unless one shall first clear away the forest and burn up the trees.

Palacios, who described this ruined city nearly three hundred years ago, saw much more than Mr. Stephens. He described "the ruins of superb edifices, built of hewn stone, which manifestly belonged to a large city." He mentions, in connection with the great wall, an enormous eagle carved in stone, which bore a square shield on its breast covered with undecipherable characters. He mentions, also, a "stone giant," and a "stone cross" with one arm broken. He saw a "plaza," circular in form, surrounded by ranges of steps or seats, which reminded him of the Coliseum at Rome, "as many as eighty ranges still remaining in some places." This "plaza" was "paved with beautiful stones, all square and well worked." Six of the great obelisks, which he described as "statues," stood in this inclosure, and in its centre was a great stone basin.

A history of Guatemala, by a writer named Huarros, states that the "Circus of Copan," as he calls the "plaza" described by Palacios, was still entire in the year 1700. He mentions gateways which led into the inclosure, and says it was surrounded on the outside by stone pyramids six yards high, near which were standing sculptured figures or obelisks. No doubt, remains of this remarkable "circus" would be found now, if the forest should be removed. What else could be found there by means of careful and thorough exploration may never be known, for the region is uninviting, the forest very difficult, and such an exploration would require much more than the means and efforts of one or two individuals.

Not very far away, in the neighboring State of Guatemala, on the right bank of the River Motagua, to which the Copan is a tributary, are the ruins called Quirigua. It is manifest that a great city once stood here. These ruins have a close resemblance to those at Copan, but they appear to be much older, for they have, to a great

Fig. 30.—Ruins of Mills.

extent, become little more than heaps of rubbish. Over a large space of ground traces of what has gone to decay are visible. Doubtless important relics of the old city are now more abundant below the surface than above it. Mr. Stephens, describing what he saw there, confines his attention chiefly to a pyramidal structure with flights of steps, and monoliths larger and higher than those at Copan, but otherwise similar. He states, however, that while they have the same general style, the sculptures are in lower relief and hardly so rich in design. One of the obelisks here is twenty feet high, five feet six inches wide, and two feet eight inches thick. The chief figures carved on it are that of a man on the front, and that of a woman on the back. The sides are covered with inscriptions similar in appearance to those at Copan. Some of the other standing obelisks are higher than this. It seems reasonable to infer that the structures at Quirigua were more ancient than those at Copan.

MITLA.

The ruins called Mitla are in the Mexican State of Oxaca, about twelve leagues east from the city of Oxaca. They are situated in the upper part of a great valley, and surrounded by a waste, uncultivated region. At the time of the Spanish Conquest they were old and much worn by time and the elements, but a very large area was then covered by remains of ancient buildings. At present only six decaying edifices and three ruined pyramids, which were very finely terraced, remain for examination, the other structures being now reduced to the last stage of decay. Figures 30 and 31 present views of some of

Fig. 31.—Great Hall at Mitla.

these structures, as given by Von Temski. Figure 32, from Charnay's photograph, shows a ruin at Mitla.

These important ruins were not described by Stephens and Catherwood. Captain Dupaix's work gives some account of them, and Désiré Charnay, who saw them since 1860, brought away photographs of some of the monuments. Four of the standing edifices are described by Dupaix as "palaces," and these, he says, "were erected with lavish magnificence; * * * they combine the solidity of the works of Egypt with the elegance of those of Greece." And he adds, "But what is most remarkable, interesting, and striking in these monuments, and which alone would be sufficient to give them the first

Fig. 73.—Ruined Palace at Mitla.

FIG. 84.—Mosaics at Mitla.

rank among all known orders of architecture, is the execution of their mosaic relievos, very different from plain mosaic, and consequently requiring more ingenious combination and greater art and labor. They are inlaid on the surface of the wall, and their duration is owing to the method of fixing the prepared stones into the stone surface, which made their union with it perfect." Figure 33, taken from Charnay's photograph, shows part of the mosaic decoration on a wall of one of the great edifices at Mitla.

The general character of the architecture and masonry is much like that seen in the structures at Palenque, but the finish of the workmanship appears to have been more artistic and admirable. These ruins are remarkable among those of the country where they are found. All who have seen them speak much as Dupaix speaks of the perfection of the masonry, the admirable design and finish of the work, and the beauty of the decorations. Their beauty, says M. Charnay, can be matched only by the monuments of Greece and Rome in their best days. One fact presented by some of the edifices at Mitla has a certain degree of historical significance. There appears to be evidence that they were occupied at some period by people less advanced in civilization than their builders. M. Charnay, describing one of them, points out this fact. He says of the structure:

"It is a bewildering maze of courts and buildings, with facings ornamented with mosaics in relief of the purest design; but under the projections are found traces of paintings wholly primitive in style, in which the right line is not even respected. These are rude figures of idols, and meandering lines that have no significance. Similar paintings appear, with the same imperfection, on every great edifice, in places which have allowed them shelter against the ravages of time. These rude designs, associated with palaces so correct in architecture, and so ornamented with panels of mosaic of such marvelous workmanship, put strange thoughts in the mind. To find the explanation of this phenomenon, must we not suppose these palaces were occupied by a race less advanced in civilization than their first builders?"

Two miles or more away from the great edifices here mentioned, toward the west, is the "Castle of Mitla." It was built on the summit of an isolated and precipitous hill of rock, which is accessible only on the east side. The whole leveled summit of this hill is inclosed by a solid wall of hewn stone twenty-one feet thick and eighteen feet high. This wall has salient and retiring angles, with curtains interposed. On the east side it is flanked by double walls. Within the inclosure are the remains of several small buildings. The field of these ruins was very large three hundred years ago. At that time it may have included this castle.

AN ASTRONOMICAL MONUMENT.

In this part of Mexico Captain Dupaix examined a peculiar ruin, of which he gave the following account: "Near the road from the village of Tlalmanalco to that called Mecameean, about three miles east of the latter, there is an isolated granite rock, which was artificially formed into a kind of pyramid with six hewn steps facing the east. The summit of this structure is a platform, or horizontal plane, well adapted to observation of the stars on every side of the hemisphere. It is almost demonstrable that this very ancient monument was exclusively devoted to astronomical observations, for on the south side of the rock are sculptured several hieroglyphical figures having relation to astronomy. The most striking figure in the group is that of a man in profile, standing erect, and directing his view to the rising stars in the sky. He holds to his eye a tube or optical instrument. Below his feet is a frieze divided into six compartments, with as many celestial signs carved on its surface." It has been already stated that finely-wrought "telescopic tubes" have been found among remains of the Mound-Builders. They were used, it seems, by the ancient people of Mexico and Central America, and they were known also in ancient Peru, where a silver figure of a man in the act of using such a tube has been discovered in one of the old tombs.

RUINS FARTHER SOUTH.

Old ruins, of which but little is known, exist in Guatemala, Honduras, San Salvador, and the more southern portion of Central America. Mr. Squier, who tells us more of them than any other explorer, says, "I heard of remains and monuments in Honduras and San Salvador equal to those of Copan in extent and interest." He mentions the ruins of Opico, near San Vincente, in San Salvador, which "cover nearly two square miles, and consist of vast terraces, ruins of edifices, circular and square towers, and subterranean galleries, all built of cut stones: a single carving has been found here on a block of stone." Remains of "immense works" exist in the district of Chontales, near the northern shore of Lake Nicaragua; and pottery found in Nicaragua "equals the best specimens of Mexico and Peru." Don José Antonio Urritia, curó of Jutiapa, gave the following account of a great ruin on a mountain in San Salvador, near the town of Comapa: it is called Cinaca-Mecallo:

"The walls, or remains of the city wall, describe an oval figure, within which roads or streets may be traced, and there are various subterranean passages and many ruined edifices. The materials of construction are chiefly thin stones, or a species of slate, united by a kind of cement which in appearance resembles melted lead." It does not appear that he made a complete examination of the monuments, but he mentions three that gained his attention, and left upon his mind a very strong impression. "The first is a temple consecrated to the sun, chiefly excavated in the solid rock, and having its entrance toward the east. On the archway of the entrance are carved representations of the sun and moon. Hieroglyphics are found in the interior. Besides the sculptured *bassi relievi*, these stones bear hieroglyphics painted with a kind of red varnish which remains unimpaired. The second is a great stone slab covered with inscriptions or hieroglyphics. The third is the figure of a wild animal sculptured on a rock or stone, of "great size."

THE RUINS IN YUCATAN.

The remains of ancient cities are abundant in the settled portion of Yucatan, which lies north of the great forest. Charnay found "the country covered with them from north to south." Stephens states, in the Preface to his work on Yucatan, that he visited "forty-four ruined cities or places" in which such remains are still found, most of which were unknown to white men, even to those inhabiting the country; and he adds that "time and the elements are hastening them to utter destruction."

Previous to the Spanish Conquest, the region known to us as Yucatan was called Maya. It is still called Maya by the natives among themselves, and this is the true name of the country. Why the Spaniards called it Yucatan is unknown, but the name is wholly arbitrary and without reason. It is said to have arisen from an odd mistake like that which occasioned the name given to one of the capes by Hernandez de Cordova. Being on the coast in 1517, he met some of the natives. Their cacique said to him, "Conex cotoch," meaning "Come to our town." The Spaniard, supposing he had mentioned the name of the place, immediately named the projecting point of land "Cape Cotoche," and it is called so still.

At that time the country was occupied by the people still known as Mayas. They all spoke the same language, which was one of a closely related family of tongues spoken in Guatemala, Chiapas, Western Honduras, and in some other districts of Central America and Mexico. Yucatan was then much more populous than at present. The people had more civilization, more regular industry, and more wealth. They were much more highly skilled in the arts of civilized life. They had cities and large towns; and dwelling-houses, built of timber and covered with thatch, like those common in England, were scattered over all the rural districts. Some of the cities now found in ruins were then inhabited. This peninsula had been the seat of an important feudal monarchy, which arose probably after the Toltecs overthrew the very ancient kingdom of Xibalba. It was broken up by a rebellion of the feudal lords about a hundred years previous to the arrival of the Spaniards. According to the Maya chronicles, its downfall occurred in the year 1420. Mayapan, the capital of this kingdom, was destroyed at that time, and never afterward inhabited.

Merida, the present capital of Yucatan, was built on the site of an ancient Maya city called Tihoo. It is stated in the old Spanish accounts of Merida that it was built on that site because there was in the ruins an abundance of building material. There is mention of two "mounds" which furnished a vast amount of hewn stone. Mr. Stephens noticed in some of the edifices stones with "sculptured figures, from the ruins of ancient buildings;" and he mentions that a portion of an ancient building, including an arch in the Maya style, was retained in the construction of the Franciscan convent.

MAYAPAN.

We shall notice only some of the principal ruins in Yucatan, beginning with Mayapan, the ancient capital. The remains of this city are situated about ten leagues, in a southern direction, from Merida. They are spread over an extensive plain, and overgrown by trees and other vegetation. The most prominent object seen by

Fig. 54.—Great Mound at Mayapan.

the approaching explorer is a great mound, 60 feet high and 100 feet square at the base. It is an imposing structure, seen through the trees, and is itself overgrown like a wooded hill. Figure 34 shows one view of this. Four stairways, in a ruinous condition, 25 feet wide, lead up to an esplanade within 6 feet of the top, which is reached by a smaller stairway. The summit is a plain stone platform 15 feet square. This, of course, was a temple. Sculptured stones are scattered around the base, and within the mound subterranean chambers have been discovered.

It is probable that the principal edifices at Mayapan were not all built wholly of stone, for they have mostly disappeared. Only one remains, a circular stone building 25 feet in diameter, which stands on a pyramidal foundation 35 feet high. This is represented in Figure 35. On the southwest side of it, on a terrace projecting from the mound, was a double row of columns without capitals, 8 feet apart. There are indications that this city was old, and that the buildings had been more than once renewed. Brasseur de Bourbourg classes some of the foundations at Mayapan with the oldest seen at Palenque and Copan. This point, however, can not be determined with sufficient accuracy to remove all doubt. Mayapan may have stood upon the foundations of a very ancient city which was several times rebuilt, but the city destroyed in 1420 could not have been as old as either Palenque or Copan.

Fig. 25.—Circular Edifice at Mayapan.

UXMAL.

The ruins of Uxmal have been regarded as the most important in Yucatan, partly on account of the edifices that remain standing, but chiefly because they have been more visited and explored than the others. It is supposed, and circumstantial evidence appears to warrant the supposition, that this city had not been wholly deserted at the time of the Spanish Conquest, although it had previously begun to be a ruin. It was wholly a ruin in 1673. The area covered by its remains is extensive. Charnay makes it a league or more in diameter; but most of the structures have fallen, and exist now only in fragments scattered over the ground. It may be that many of them were not built wholly of hewn stone, and had not "Egyptian solidity" with their other characteristics.

The most important of those remaining was named "Casa del Gobernador" by the Spaniards. It is 320 feet long, and was built of hewn stone laid in mortar or cement. The faces of the walls are smooth up to the cornice. Then follows, on all the four sides, " one solid mass of rich, complicated, and elaborately sculptured ornaments, forming a sort of arabesque." Figure 36 gives a view of the south end of this edifice, but no engraving can show all the details of the ornamentation.

This building has eleven doorways in front, and one at each end, all having wooden lintels, which have fallen. The two principal rooms are 60 feet long, and from 11 to 13 feet wide. This structure is long and narrow

132 *Ancient America.*

Fig. 36.—Casa del Gobernador, Uxmal.

The arrangement and number of the rooms are shown in the following ground plan of the building (Figure 37):

Fig. 37.—Ground Plan of Casa del Gobernador

Fig. 86.—Double-headed Figure, Casa del Gobernador.

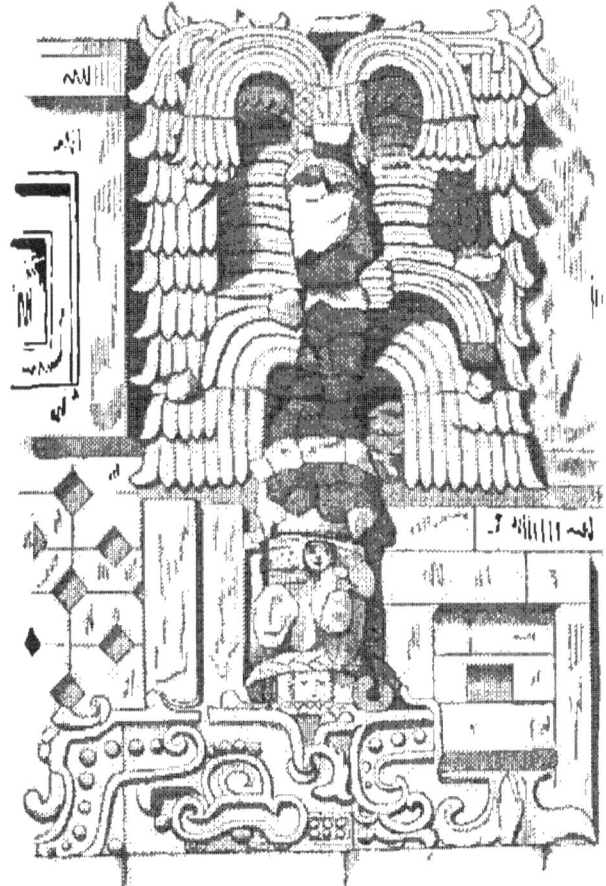

Fig. 22.—Decorations over Doorway, Casa del Gobernador.

It stands on the summit of one of the grandest of the terraced foundations. This foundation, like all the others, is pyramidal. It has three terraces. The lowest is 3 feet high, 15 wide, and 575 long; the second is 20 feet high, 275 wide, and 545 long; the third, 19 feet high, 30 wide, and 360 long. Structures formerly existed on the second terrace, remains of which are visible. At the northwest corner one of them still shows its dilapidated walls, portions of them being sufficiently complete to show what they were. This edifice was 94 feet long and 34 wide. It seems to have been finely finished in a style more simple than that of the great "casa" on the upper terrace. The figures of turtles sculptured along the upper edge of the cornice have given it the current designation, "House of the Turtles." Sculptured monuments have been found buried in the soil of the second terrace. The opening of a small, low mound situated on it brought to view the double-headed figure shown in No. 38. Figure 39 shows part of the sculptured decoration over the centre doorway of Casa del Gobernador.

Another important edifice at Uxmal has been named "Casa de las Monjas," House of the Nuns. It stands on a terraced foundation, and is arranged around a quadrangular court-yard 258 feet one way and 214 the other. The front structure is 279 feet long, and has a gateway in the centre 10 feet 8 inches wide leading into the court, and four doors on each side of it. The outer face of the wall, above the cornice, is ornamented with sculptures. The terrace without and within the inclosure was found covered with a very dense growth of vegeta-

tion, which it was necessary to clear away before the
walls could be carefully examined. All the doorways,
save those in front, open on the court. Mr. Stephens
found the four great façades fronting the court-yard
"ornamented from one end to the other with the richest
and most intricate carving known to the builders of Uxmal, presenting a scene of strange magnificence which
surpasses any other now seen among its ruins." The

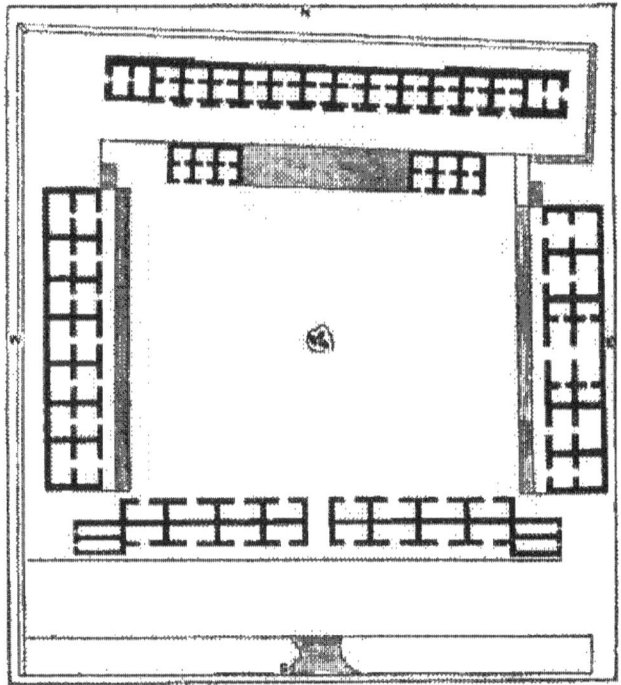

Fig. 40.—Ground Plan of Las Monjas, Uxmal.

long outer structure, on the side facing the entrance, had high turret-like elevations over each of its thirteen doorways, all covered with sculptured ornaments. This building appears to have inclosed another of older date. Figure 40 shows the ground plan of "Las Monjas."

Other less important edifices in the ruins of Uxmal have been described by explorers, some of which stand on high pyramidal mounds; and inscriptions are found here, but they are not so abundant as at Palenque and Copan.

KABAH.

The ruins known as Kabah are on the site of what must have been one of the most imposing and important of the more ancient cities. Here the most conspicuous object is a stone-faced mound 180 feet square at the base, with a range of ruined apartments at the bottom. Three or four hundred yards from this mound is a terraced foundation 20 feet high and 200 by 142 in extent, on which stand the remains of a great edifice. At the right of the esplanade before it is a "high range of ruined structures overgrown with trees, with an immense back wall on the outer line of the esplanade perpendicular to the bottom of the terrace." On the left is another range of ruined buildings, and in the centre a stone inclosure 27 feet square and 7 feet high, with sculptures and inscriptions around the base. Some of the ornamentation of this building has been described in the strongest terms of admiration. Mr. Stephens said of it, "The cornice running over the doorways, tried by the severest rules of art recognized among us, would embellish the architecture of any known era." At Uxmal the walls were smooth below the cornice; here they are covered with decorations from top to bottom.

This field of ruins is extensive, and only a portion of it has been examined. It is so overgrown that exploration is very difficult. The buildings and mounds are much decayed, and they seem to be very old. It is believed that ruined edifices of which nothing is known are hidden among the trees in places which no explorer has approached. Mr. Stephens gave the first account of Kabah, and described three other important edifices besides that already named. One of these he thought was, when entire, the most imposing structure at Kabah. It was 147 feet long by 106 wide, and had three distinct stories, each successive story being smaller than that below it. Another, standing on the upper terrace of an elevated foundation 170 feet long by 110 broad, was 164 feet in length, and comparatively narrow. It is mentioned as a peculiarity of this edifice that it had pillars in its doorways, used as supports. The other, found standing on a terrace, is also long and narrow, and has a comparatively plain front.

Remains of other buildings are visible, but in all cases they are so completely in ruins as to be little more than heaps of débris. Some of the ruins in the woods beyond that part of the field which is most accessible, are visible from the great mound described. A resolute attempt to penetrate the forest brought the explorers in view of great edifices standing on an elevated terrace estimated to be 800 feet long by 100 feet wide. The decorations seemed to have been abundant and very rich, but the structures were in a sad state of dilapidation. One remarkable monument found at Kabah resembles a triumphal arch. It stands by itself on a ruined mound apart from the other structures. It is described as a "lonely arch, having a span of 14 feet," rising on the field of ruins "in solitary grandeur." Figure 41 gives a view of it.

Fig. 41.—Ruined Arch at Kabah.

Kabah was an ancient city. The ruins are old, and the city may have belonged to the first age of the Maya period.

CHICHEN-ITZA.

The ruins of Chichen-Itza are situated east of Mayapan, about half way between the eastern and western coasts of the peninsula of Yucatan. A public road runs through the space of ground over which they are spread. The area covered by them is something less than a mile in diameter. The general character of the ruined structures found here is in every respect like that shown by ruins already described.

One of the great buildings at this place has a rude, unornamental exterior, and does not stand on an artificial terrace, although the ground before it was excavated so as to give the appearance of an elevated foundation. It is one hundred and forty-nine feet long by forty-eight deep. Its special peculiarity consists of a stone lintel, in a very dark inner room, which has an inscription and a sculptured figure on the under side. The writing closely resembles that seen at Palenque and Copan. Was this sculptured stone made originally for the place it now occupies, or was it taken from the ruins of some older city which flourished and went to decay before Chichen-Itza was built?

Another structure seen here closely resembles Las Monjas at Uxmal, and bears the same name, but it differs somewhat from the Uxmal Monjas in arrangement. In the descriptions, special mention is made of "the richness and beauty" of its ornaments.

A noticeable edifice connected with the Monjas, called the "Church," is 26 feet long, 14 deep, 31 high, and has three cornices, the spaces between them being covered with carved ornaments. There is but one room in it. One of the most picturesque ruins at Chichen-Itza is circular in form, and stands on the upper level of a double-terraced platform. It is 22 feet in diameter, and has four doors, which face the cardinal points. Above the cornice it slopes gradually almost to a point, and the top is about 60 feet above the ground. The grand staircase of 20 steps, leading up to this building, is 45 feet wide, and has a sort of balustrade formed of the entwined bodies of huge serpents. At some distance from this is the ruined structure known as the "Casa Colorada," or Red House. This is shown in Figure 42.

Fig. 42.—Casa Colorada.

It is 43 feet long by 23 deep, and stands on a platform 62 feet long by 55 wide. It was ornamented above the cornice, but the decorations are much defaced by decay. A stone tablet extending the whole length of the back wall, inside, is covered by an inscription.

A remarkable structure is found at this place, which Mr. Stephens called the "Gymnasium, or Tennis Court." It consists of two immense parallel walls 274 feet long, 30 thick, and 120 apart. On elevations facing the two ends of the open space between them, 100 feet from the ends of the walls, stand two edifices much ruined, but showing, in their remains, that they were richly ornamented. Midway in the length of the walls, facing each other, and 20 feet above the ground, are two massive stone rings or circles 4 feet in diameter, each having in the centre a hole 1 foot and 7 inches in diameter. On the borders around these holes two entwined serpents are sculptured, as seen in Figure 43.

There was a similar structure in the old city of Mexico, and remains of one like it are found at Mayapan. They were, probably, used for games of some kind. Among the other ruins at Chichen-Itza are the remains of a lofty edifice which has two high ranges or stories. On the outside the ornamentation is simple and tasteful, but the walls of its chambers are very elaborately decorated, mostly with sculptured designs, which seem to have been painted. In one of the upper rooms Mr. Stephens found a beam of sapote wood used as a lintel, which was covered with very elegantly carved decorations. The walls of this room were covered, from the

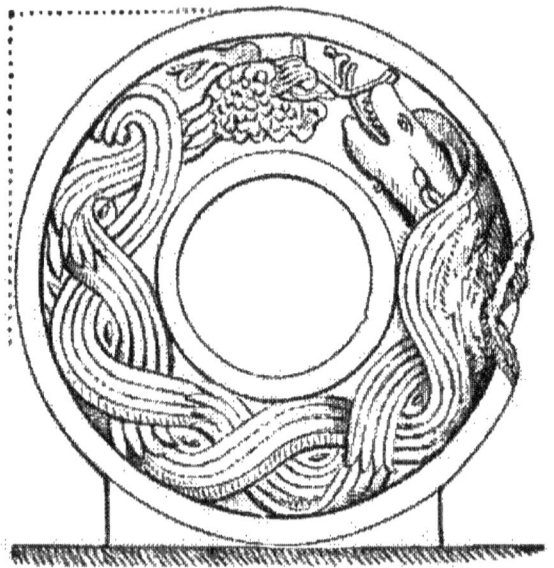

Fig. 43.—Great Stone Ring.

bottom to the top of the arched ceiling, with painted designs similar to those seen in the Mexican "picture writing." Decay had mutilated these "pictures," but the colors were still bright. There are indications that painting was generally used by the aboriginal builders, even on their sculptures. The colors seen in this room were green, red, yellow, blue, and reddish-brown. Another edifice, standing on a high mound, is reached by means of the usual great stairway, which begins at the bottom, with a sort of balustrade on each side, the ends of which are stone figures of heads of immense serpents.

Not far from this is a singular ruin, consisting of groups of small columns standing in rows five abreast, the tallest being not more than six feet high. Many of them have fallen. It is impossible to determine how they were used, or what they mean.

OTHER RUINS IN YUCATAN.

Izamal, Labna, Zayi, and some of the other ruins are sufficiently important for special notice; but they present every where the same characteristics, differing a little in the style or method of ornamentation. At Labna there is among the ruins an ancient gateway, beautiful in design and construction, a view of which is given in the Frontispiece. The best account of some of the other ruins on this peninsula can be found in the volumes of Mr. Stephens, entitled "Incidents of Travel in Yucatan." At Zayi there is a singular building, which, as seen at a distance by Mr. Stephens, "had the appearance of a New England factory." But what seemed to be a "factory" is, in fact, nothing more than a massive wall with oblong openings, which runs along the middle of the roof, and rises thirty feet above it. The building was below this wall, but the front part of it had fallen. Among the remains at Xcoch is the great mound represented in Figure 44.

There is a remarkable ruin at Ake, at the south, which deserves mention. Here, on the summit of a great mound, very level, and 225 feet by 50 in extent, stand 36 shafts or columns, in three parallel rows. The columns are about 15 feet high and 4 feet square. The

Fig. 44.—Great Mound at Xcoch.

ruins of Ake, which cover a great space, are ruder and more massive than most of the others. The island of Cozumel and the adjacent coast of Yucatan were populous when the Spaniards first went there, but the great towns then inhabited are now in ruins.

Water is scarce on this peninsula, and a sufficient supply is not obtained without considerable difficulty. The ancient inhabitants provided for this lack of water by constructing aguadas or artificial ponds. These, or many of them, doubtless, are as old as the oldest of the ruined

cities. Intelligence, much skill in masonry, and much
labor were required to construct them. They were paved
with several courses of stone laid in cement, and in their
bottoms wells or cavities were constructed. More than
forty such wells were found in the bottom of one of these
aguadas at Galal, which has been repaired and restored
to use. A section of the bottom of this aguada is shown
in Figure 45. In some places long subterranean passa-

Fig. 45.—Bottom of an Aguada.

ges lead down to pools of water, which are used in the
dry season. One of these subterranean reservoirs, and
the cavernous passage leading to it, are shown in Figure
46. The reservoir is 450 feet below the surface of the
ground, and the passage leading to it is about 1400 feet
long. Branching passages, not shown, lead to two or
three other basins of water.

The wooden lintels, which are common in Yucatan,

do not appear in the other ruins, and there is a difference in the style of ornamentation between those at

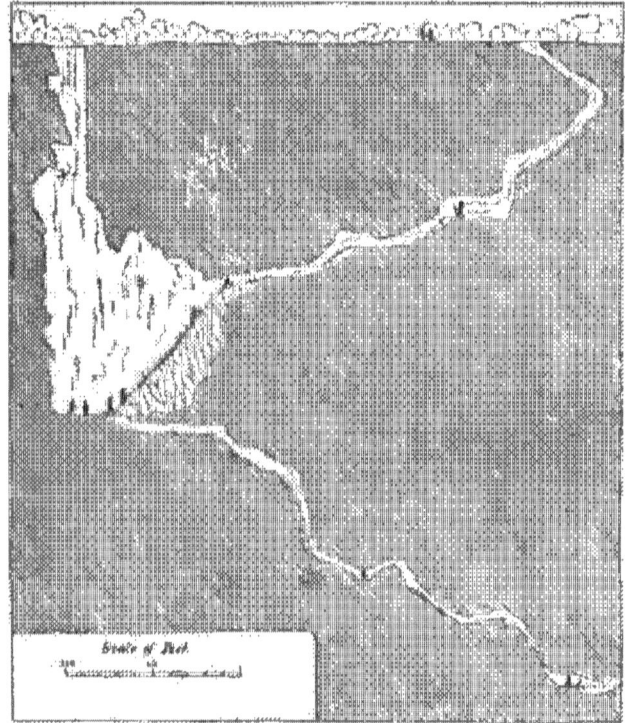

Fig. 66.—Subterranean Reservoir.

Palenque or Copan, for instance, and those at Uxmal, but every where the architecture is regulated by the same idea, the differences indicating nothing more than different periods and different phases of development in the history of the same people.

Some of the great edifices in these old ruins, such as the "Palace" at Palenque, and the "Casa del Gobernador" at Uxmal, remind us of the "communal buildings" of the Pueblos, and yet there is a wide difference between them. They are not alike either in character or purpose, although such great buildings as the "Palace" may have been designed for the occupation of several families. There is no indication that "communal" residences were ever common in this part of the country. At the time of the Conquest the houses of the people were ordinary family dwellings, made of wood, and we may reasonably suppose this fashion of building was handed down from the earlier ages. Herrera, who supposed, mistakenly, that all the great stone edifices were

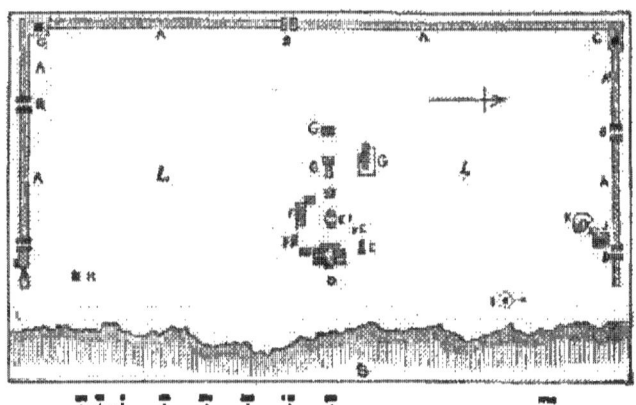

Fig. 47.—Plan of the Walls at Tuluum.

temples, said, in his account of Yucatan, "There were so many and such stately stone buildings that it was amazing; and the greatest wonder was that, having no use of any metal, they were able to raise such structures, which seem to have been temples; for their houses were all of timber, and thatched." But they had the use of metals, and they had the art of making some of them admirable for use in cutting stone and carving wood.

Fig. 48.—Watch-tower at Tuloom.

Among the buildings of later date are some of those on the western coast, which were still inhabited three hundred and fifty years ago. The city of Tuloom was inhabited then. Figure 47 shows a ground plan of the walls of this city, with the position of some of the ruined monuments.

Within the walls are remains of finely constructed buildings on elevated foundations, none of them, however, very large. One of them had a wooden roof, and timber seems to have been considerably used here. The walls still standing were made of hewn stone. Remains of stone edifices exist all along this coast, but the whole region is now covered by a dense growth of trees and other vegetation. Tuloom was seen in 1518 by Grijalva, who sailed along the coast. At that time the island of Cozumel, where noteworthy ruins are found, was inhabited by many people. Figure 48 shows one of the watchtowers on the walls of Tuloom.

VI.

ANTIQUITY OF THE RUINS.

The Mexican and Central American ruins make it certain that in ancient times an important civilization existed in that part of the continent, which must have begun at a remote period in the past. If they have any significance, this must be accepted as an ascertained fact. A large proportion of them had been forgotten in the forests, or become mythical and mysterious, long before the arrival of the Spaniards.

In 1520, three hundred and fifty years ago, the forest which so largely covers Yucatan, Guatemala, and Chiapa was growing as it grows now; yes, four hundred and fifty years ago, for it was there a century previous to this date, when, the Maya kingdom being broken up, one of its princes fled into this forest with a portion of his people, the Itzas, and settled at Lake Peten. It was the same then as now. How many additional centuries it had existed no one can tell. If its age could be told, it would still be necessary to consider that the ruins hidden in it are much older than the forest, and that the period of civilization they represent closed long before it was established.

In the ages previous to the beginning of this immense forest, the region it covers was the seat of a civilization which grew up to a high degree of development, flourished a long time, and finally declined, until its cities were deserted, and its cultivated fields left to the wild influences of nature. It may be safely assumed that both the forest-covered ruins and the forest itself are far older than the Aztec period; but who can tell how much older? Copan, first discovered and described three hundred years ago, was then as strange to the natives dwelling near it as the old Chaldean ruins are to the Arabs who wander over the wasted plains of Lower Mesopotamia. Native tradition had forgotten its history and become silent in regard to it. How long had ruined Copan been in this condition? No one can tell. Manifestly it was forgotten, left buried in the forest without recollection of its history, long before Montezuma's people, the Aztecs, rose to power; and it is easily understood that this old city had an important history previous to that unknown time in the past when war, revolution, or some other agency of destruction put an end to its career and left it to become what it is now.

Moreover, these old ruins, in all cases, show us only the cities last occupied in the periods to which they belong. Doubtless others still older preceded them; and, besides, it can be seen that some of the ruined cities which can now be traced were several times renewed by reconstructions. We must consider, also, that building magnificent cities is not the first work of an original civilization. The development was necessarily gradual. Its first period was more or less rude. The art of building and ornamenting such edifices arose slowly. Many ages must have been required to develop such admirable skill in masonry and ornamentation. Therefore the period between the beginning of this mysterious development of civilized life and the first builders who used cut stone laid in mortar and cement, and covered their work with beautifully sculptured ornaments and inscriptions, must have been very long.

We have no measure of the time, no clew to the old dates, nothing whatever, beyond such considerations as I have stated, to warrant even a vague hypothesis. It can be seen clearly that the beginning of this old civilization was much older than the earliest great cities, and, also, that these were much more ancient than the time when any of the later built or reconstructed cities whose relics still exist, were left to decay. If we suppose Palenque to have been deserted some six hundred years previous to the Spanish Conquest, this date will carry us back only to the last days of its history as an inhabited city. Beyond it, in the distant past, is a vast period, in which the civilization represented by Palenque was developed, made capable of building such cities, and then carried on through the many ages during which cities became numerous, flourished, grew old, and gave place to others, until the long history of Palenque itself began.

Those who have sought to discredit what is told of the Aztec civilization and the empire of Montezuma have never failed to admit fully the significance of Copan, Palenque, and Mitla. One or two writers, pursuing the assumption that the barbarous tribes at the north and the old Mexicans were of the same race, and substantially the same people, have undertaken to give us the history of Montezuma's empire "entirely rewritten," and show that his people were "Mexican savages." In their hands Montezuma is transformed into a barbarous Indian chief, and the city of Mexico becomes a rude Indian village, situated among the islands and lagoons of an everglade which afforded unusual facilities " for fishing and snaring birds." One goes so far as to maintain this with considerable vehemence and amusing unconsciousness of absurdity. He is sure that Montezuma was nothing more than the principal chief of a parcel of wild Indian tribes, and that the Pueblos are wild Indians changed to their present condition by Spanish influence. There is something in this akin to lunacy.

But this topic will receive more attention in another place. I bring it to view here because those who maintain so strangely that the Aztecs were Indian savages, admit all that is claimed for the wonderful ruins at the south, and give them a very great antiquity. They maintain, however, that the civilization represented by these ruins was brought to this continent in remote pre-historic times by the people known as Phœnicians, and their method of finding the Phœnicians at Palenque, Copan, and every where else, is similar in character and value to that by which they transform the Aztec empire into a rude confederacy of wild Indians.

DISTINCT ERAS TRACED.

It is a point of no little interest that these old constructions belong to different periods in the past, and represent somewhat different phases of civilization. Uxmal, which is supposed to have been partly inhabited when the Spaniards arrived in the country, is plainly much more modern than Copan or Palenque. This is easily traced in the ruins. Its edifices were finished in a different style, and show fewer inscriptions. Round pillars, somewhat in the Doric style, are found at Uxmal, but none like the square, richly-carved pillars, bearing inscriptions, discovered in some of the other ruins. Copan and Palenque, and even Kabah, in Yucatan, may have been very old cities, if not already old ruins, when Uxmal was built. Accepting the reports of explorers as correct, there is evidence in the ruins that Quirigua is older than Copan, and that Copan is older than Palenque. The old monuments in Yucatan represent several distinct epochs in the ancient history of that peninsula. Some of them are kindred to those hidden in the great forest, and remind us more of Palenque than of Uxmal. Among those described, the most modern, or most of these, are in Yucatan; they belong to the time when the kingdom of the Mayas flourished. Many of the others belong to ages previous to the rise of this kingdom; and in ages still earlier, ages older than the great forest, there were other cities, doubtless, whose remains have perished utterly, or were long ago removed for use in the later constructions.

The evidence of repeated reconstructions in some of
the cities before they were deserted has been pointed
out by explorers. I have quoted what Charnay says of
it in his description of Mitla. At Palenque, as at Mitla,
the oldest work is the most artistic and admirable. Over
this feature of the monuments, and the manifest signs of
their difference in age, the attention of investigators has
lingered in speculation. They find in them a significance which is stated as follows by Brasseur de Bourbourg: "Among the edifices forgotten by time in the
forests of Mexico and Central America, we find architectural characteristics so different from each other, that it
is as impossible to attribute them all to the same people
as to believe they were all built at the same epoch." In
his view, "the substructions at Mayapan, some of those
at Tulha, and a great part of those at Palenque," are
among the older remains. These are not the oldest
cities whose remains are still visible, but they may have
been built, in part, upon the foundations of cities much
more ancient.

NOTHING PERISHABLE LEFT.

No well considered theory of these ruins can avoid the
conclusion that most of them are very ancient, and that,
to find the origin of the civilization they represent, we
must go far back into the "deeps of antiquity." On all
the fields of desolation where they exist, every thing perishable has disappeared. Wooden lintels are mentioned, but these can hardly be regarded as constituting an
exception when the character of the wood, and the cir-

cumstances that contributed to their preservation, are considered. Moreover, wooden lintels seem to have been peculiar to Yucatan, where many of the great edifices were constructed in the later times, and some of them of perishable materials. Every where in the older ruins, nothing remains but the artificial mounds and foundations of earth, the stone, the cement, the stucco hard as marble, and other imperishable materials used by the builders.

If the edifices had all been made of wood, there would now be nothing to show us that the older cities had ever existed. Every trace of them would have been obliterated long before our time, and most of them would have disappeared entirely long before the country was seen by the Spaniards. The places where they stood, with no relics save the mounds and pyramidal platforms, would resemble the works of our Mound-Builders, and not a few "sound historical critics" would consider it in the highest degree absurd to suggest that cities with such structures have ever existed there. Under the circumstances supposed, how wisely skepticism could talk against a suggestion of this kind at Copan, Mitla, or Palenque! and how difficult it would be to find a satisfactory answer to its reasonings! Nevertheless, those mysterious structures have not wholly disappeared, and we can easily understand that there was a time when large areas connected with them were covered with buildings of a less durable character.

I have referred to a writer who maintains, with more vehemence than candor, that the Aztecs, and all the other people found in the country, were "savages" not greatly different from the wild Indians farther north, while he admits the significance and great antiquity of these ruins. His conception of their antiquity is somewhat extreme, for he says they must have existed "for thousands of years" when the Spaniards arrived. If he had maintained that civilized communities were there "thousands of years" previous to that time, developing the skill in architecture, decoration, and writing, to which the monuments bear witness, it might be possible to agree with him. Some of us, however, would probably stipulate that he should not count too many "thousands," nor claim a similar antiquity for the ruins now visible. It is not easy to suppose that any of these old monuments, with their well-preserved sculptures and inscriptions, represent the first period of the ancient history they suggest, nor that they have existed as ruins many "thousands of years," for the climate of Mexico and Central America does not preserve such remains like that of Egypt.

Nevertheless, some of them must be very old. The forest established since the ruin began, the entire disappearance of every thing more perishable than stone, the utter oblivion which veiled their history in the time of Montezuma, and probably long previous to his time, all these facts bear witness to their great antiquity. In many of them, as at Quirigua and Kabah, the stone structures have become masses of débris; and even at Copan, Palenque, and Mitla, only a few of them are sufficiently well preserved to show us what they were in the great days of their history. Meanwhile, keep in mind that the ruined cities did not begin their present condition until the civilization that created them had declined; and, also, that if we could determine exactly the date when they were deserted and left to decay, we should only reach that point in the past where their history as inhabited cities was brought to a close.

Take Copan, for instance. This city may have become a ruin during the time of the Toltecs, which began long before the Christian era, and ended some five or six centuries probably before the country was invaded by Cortez. It was built before their time, for the style of writing, and many features of the architecture and ornamentation, show the workmanship of their predecessors, judging by the historical intimations found in the old books and traditions. We may suppose it to have been an old city at the time of the Toltec invasion, although not one of the first cities built by that more ancient and more cultivated people by whom this old American civilization was originated. The present condition of the monuments at Quirigua is still more suggestive of great age.

"THE OLDEST OF CIVILIZATIONS."

Some investigators, who have given much study to the antiquities, traditions, old books, and probable geological history of Mexico and Central America, believe that the first civilization the world ever saw appeared in this part of Ancient America, or was immediately connected with it. They hold that the human race first rose to civilized life in America, which is, geologically, the oldest of the continents; and that, ages ago, the portion of this continent on which the first civilizers appeared was sunk beneath the waters of the Atlantic Ocean. Usually the ingulfing of this portion of the land is supposed to have been effected by some tremendous convulsion of nature; and there is appeal to recollections of such a catastrophe, said to have been preserved in the old books of Central America, and also in those of Egypt, from which Solon received an account of the lost Atlantis.

According to this hypothesis, the American continent formerly extended from Mexico, Central America, and New Granada far into the Atlantic Ocean toward Europe and Africa, covering all the space now occupied by the Caribbean Sea, the Gulf of Mexico, and the West India islands, and going far beyond them toward the east and northeast. This lost portion of the continent was the Atlantis of which the old annals of Egypt told so much in the time of Solon, as we learn from Plato; and it was the original seat of the first human civilization, which, after the great cataclysm, was renewed and perpetuated in the region where we now trace the mysterious remains of ancient cities. Those desiring to know what can be said in support of this view of Ancient America must read the later volumes of Brasseur de Bourbourg, especially his "Quatre Lettres sur le Mexique," and his "Sources de l'Histoire Primitive du Mexique," etc. He is not a perspicuous writer; he uses but little system in treating the subject, and he introduces many fanciful speculations which do more to embarrass than to help the discussion; but those who read the books patiently can find and bring together all that relates to the point in question, and consider it in their own way. They can also find it set forth and defended in a small volume by George Catlin, entitled "The Lifted and Subsided Rocks of America," published in London, not long since, by Trübner and Company.

I shall give more attention to this theory in the next chapter. I refer to it here on account of the very great antiquity it claims for the ancient American civilization. It represents that the advanced human development whose crumbling monuments are studied at Copan, Mitla, and Palenque antedates every thing else in the human period of our globe, excepting, perhaps, an earlier time of barbarism and pastoral simplicity; that its history goes back through all the misty ages of pre-historic time to an unknown date previous to the beginning of such civilization in any part of the Old World. It is hardly possible to make it more ancient.

AMERICAN CITIES SEEN BY TYRIANS.

The view just stated touches the imagination and stirs the feelings like a genuine "wonder story;" but this should not be allowed to deny it a fair hearing. Those who reject it should disprove it before they hasten to pronounce it "absurd" and "impossible," else it may be suspected that their accustomed views of antiquity are due more to education, and to the habit of following a given fashion of thinking, than to actual reflection. It needs demonstration; and we may reasonably suggest that, in the present state of our knowledge of the past, demonstration is impossible. Meanwhile, a clear historical record appears to make it certain that flourishing towns and cities were seen and visited in America three thousand years ago, by persons who went to them across the Atlantic.

It is said, more or less clearly, by more than one Greek writer, that the Phœnicians and Carthaginians knew the way to a continent beyond the Atlantic. One fact preserved in the annals of Tyrian commerce, and mentioned by several ancient writers, is related by Diodorus Siculus very particularly as a matter of authentic history. His narration begins with the following statement:

"Over against Africa lies a very great island, in the vast ocean, many days' sail from Libya westward. The soil there is very fruitful, a great part whereof is mountainous, but much likewise champaign, which is the most sweet and pleasant part, for it is watered by several navigable streams, and beautified with many gardens of pleasure planted with divers sorts of trees and an abundance of orchards. The towns are adorned with stately buildings and banqueting houses pleasantly situated in their gardens and orchards." The great ruins in Yucatan, and elsewhere in Mexico and Central America, bear witness that there was, anciently, such a country as this, across the ocean, "many days' sail from Libya westward;" but Diodorus Siculus lived before the Christian era, and how was this known to him and others more than fifteen hundred years before America was discovered by Columbus? He tells us as follows: "The Phœnicians

(Tyrians) having found out the coasts beyond the Pillars of Hercules, sailed along by the coast of Africa. One of their ships, on a sudden, was driven by a furious storm far off into the main ocean. After they had lain under this violent tempest many days, they at length arrived at this island."

This reminds us of the constrained voyage of Biarni, the Northman, from Iceland to the coast of Massachusetts, in the year 985 A.D.* He, too, was storm-driven "many days," and in this way forced to the discovery of New England. He started for Greenland, and finally reached it by way of Martha's Vineyard and Cape Cod. The tempest-driven ship of the Tyrians must have been carried to the West Indies, and to the coast of Honduras or Yucatan, where the Tyrians saw the gardens, cities, and stately edifices. The description of what they saw brings to mind similar accounts of what was seen in Yucatan by the Spaniards, when they began to sail along the coast of that peninsula in the beginning of the sixteenth century; Juan Diaz de Solis and Vincente Yañez Pinçon in 1506, and Hernandez de Cordova in 1517. They, too, saw handsome towns and stately buildings.

This undesigned voyage of the Tyrian ship seems to have been made previous to the building of Gadir, or Gades. Perhaps they made other voyages to that region, but it was a custom of the Phœnicians to be very secret in regard to the methods and paths of their commerce. A complete history of their commerce and navigation from the earliest times would unquestionably give

* See Appendix A.

us views of the past quite as startling to the prevalent assuming, unreasoning habits of belief, or rather disbelief, concerning antiquity, as that hypothesis of Atlantis and the earliest civilization. What is told by Diodorus authorizes us to suppose that the Tyrians who went across the Atlantic as described beheld some of the ancient American cities which are now found in ruins, for it is certain that nothing of the kind existed any where else "many days' sail from Libya [Northern Africa] westward." Their voyage was made more than eleven hundred years previous to the Christian era. If the old Central American books may be trusted, this was not very long previous to the beginning of the Toltec domination.

Beyond this date, the history of the "Colhuas," who are described as the original civilizers, must have covered a very long period; how long we may imagine, but can not know. Gadir, now Cadiz, founded eleven hundred years previous to the Christian era, is still an inhabited city; it has been several times reconstructed, but never deserted. When it was built, Tartessus, then a very old city, still existed, although it was in ruins long before Christ appeared. How long had Palenque been in existence when that Tyrian ship was driven across the Atlantic? And how long had that region been a region of cities and civilization? There is no history which can answer these questions.

VII.

WHENCE CAME THAT OLD CIVILIZATION?

VARIOUS theories, some of them very wild and irrational, have been advanced to explain the origin of what is seen in these relics of Ancient America. If it had been the fashion to explore and study them as their importance deserves, as Egypt and Nineveh have been explored and studied, our knowledge of them would now be much more extensive and valuable, and it might be possible to go farther toward a solution of the problem they present. But not many persons have sought to explore and understand these remains, and not more than two or three have really sought in earnest to examine the old traditions and books of the country. The abundant inscriptions at Palenque fade in their forest solitude while waiting for the Champollion who shall interpret their mysteries. Something is known, but we have no history of these old cities, no authentic historical record of the people who built them. Therefore theorizing has very naturally been stimulated to great activity, and most of this theorizing has been regulated by the old, unreasoning assumption that civilization found in any place, especially in the olden times, must have been brought and established there as a foreign production. Generally the hypotheses used in this case have presumed as a matter of course that the original civilizers came to this continent from Europe or Asia.

THE "LOST TRIBES OF ISRAEL."

One of these theories is (or was), that the original civilizers of Mexico and Central America were the "lost ten tribes of Israel." This extremely remarkable explanation of the mystery was devised very early, and it has been persistently defended by some persons, although nothing can be more unwarranted or more absurd. It was put forward by the Spanish monks who first established missions in the country, a class of men to whom the world is indebted for a great variety of amazing contributions to the literature of hagiology; and the same men, in a way equally conclusive, explained the sculptured crosses found in the old ruins by assuming that the Gospel was preached in America by St. Thomas. Lord Kingsborough adopted their views, and gave up nearly the whole of one of his immense volumes on Mexican Antiquities to an elaborate digest of all that had been written to explain and support these absurdities. Others have maintained this Israelitish hypothesis without deeming it necessary to estimate in a reasonable way what was possible to those Israelites.

According to this truly monkish theory, the "lost ten tribes of Israel" left Palestine, Syria, Assyria, or whatever country they dwelt in at the time, traversed the whole extent of Asia, crossed over into America at Behring's Strait, went down the Pacific coast, and established a wonderful civilization in that part of the continent

where the great ruins are found. The kingdom of the
ten tribes was destroyed not long previous to the year
700 B.C. How many years are allowed, after their escape from captivity, for this unparalleled journey, has
not yet been ascertained. But, if such a journey had
been possible, it would have resulted in utter barbarism
rather than any notable phase of civilized life. Even
the Jews who remained faithful to Moses, although important on account of their scriptures and their religion,
were not remarkable for civilization. They were incapable of building their own Temple without aid from
the Tyrians. Moreover, there is not any where either a
fact, a suggestion, or a circumstance of any kind to show
that the "lost ten tribes" ever left the countries of Southwestern Asia, where they dwelt after the destruction of
their kingdom. They were "lost" to the Jewish nation
because they rebelled, apostatized, and, after their subjugation by the Assyrians in 721 B.C., were to a great extent absorbed by other peoples in that part of Asia.
Some of them probably were still in Palestine when
Christ appeared. This wild notion, called a theory,
scarcely deserves so much attention. It is a lunatic fancy, possible only to men of a certain class, which in our
time does not multiply.

THE "MALAY" THEORY.

Another hypothesis, much less improbable, though not
satisfactory, is that civilization was brought to America
in ancient times by the Malays. There was a great isl-
and empire of the Malays, whose history extended far

back into pre-historic times, how far back can not now be known. It was still in existence when the Portuguese first went to India around the Cape of Good Hope; and we have several accounts of this empire written by travelers who saw and described it six hundred years before this first Indian voyage of the Portuguese was undertaken. El Mas'údí, who was one of these travelers, used very strong terms to describe its extent, intelligence, and power. Speaking of its sovereign, he said, "The islands under his sceptre are so numerous that the fastest sailing vessel is not able to go round them in two years," implying that his sway was acknowledged by the island world over a large portion of the Pacific. This Malayan empire was maritime and commercial; it had fleets of great ships; and there is evidence that its influence reached most of the Pacific islands. This is shown by the fact that dialects of the Malay language have been found in most of these islands as far in this direction as Easter Island. The language of the Sandwich Islanders, for instance, is Malayan, and has a close relationship to that now spoken in the Malay islands.

The metropolis of this great empire was in the island of Java, where old ruins still bear witness to the former "civilization, wealth, and splendor" celebrated by El Mas'údí. Mr. A. R. Wallace, in his work on the Malay Archipelago, says, "Few Englishmen are aware of the number and beauty of the architectural remains in Java. They have never been popularly illustrated or described, and it will therefore take most persons by surprise to learn that they far surpass those of Central America, perhaps even those of India." The purpose of his visit to the island did not allow him to explore ruins, but he describes some of them. He saw what still remains of an ancient city called "Modjo-pahit," and says, "There were two lofty brick masses, apparently the sides of a gateway. The extreme perfection and beauty of the brick-work astonished me. The bricks are exceedingly fine and hard, with sharp angles and true surfaces. They were laid with great exactness, without visible mortar or cement, yet somehow fastened together so that the joints are hardly perceptible, and sometimes the two surfaces coalesce in a most incomprehensible manner. Such admirable brick-work I have never seen before or since. There was no sculpture here, but abundance of bold projections and finely-worked mouldings. Traces of buildings exist for many miles in every direction, and almost every road and pathway shows a foundation of brickwork beneath it, the paved roads of the old city." In other places he saw sculptures and beautifully carved figures in high relief.

The Malays still read and write, have some literature, and retain many of the arts and usages of civilization, but they are now very far below the condition indicated by these ruins, and described by El Mas'údí, who traveled among them a thousand years ago. It is by no means improbable that their ships visited the western coast of America, and traded with the ancient Mexicans and Peruvians in the days of their greatest power and activity. It is not easy to believe they could fail to do so after taking such control of Easter Island as to leave their language there; and, according to the old traditions of both Mexico and Peru, the Pacific coast in both countries was anciently visited by a foreign people who came in ships. But they did not come to America as civilizers; there is nothing Malayan in either the antiquities or the ancient speech of these countries.

What is known of the former great condition and power of the Malays furnishes important suggestions relative to the ancient history of the islands of Eastern Asia and the Pacific Ocean,* as well as those of the Indian Ocean.

The people who inhabit the eastern side of Formosa, it is said, use a Malay dialect, and have no resemblance whatever to the Mongols. Who can fully explain the little known Ainos, who formerly occupied the whole, or nearly the whole of Japan? The unmistakable traces of Malay influence every where in the islands of the Pacific can have but one meaning. The Malays formerly sailed on that ocean, occupied its islands, and doubtless visited America.

That there was communication between Eastern Asia and America in very ancient times, through the Malays or otherwise, is in a high degree probable. This continent was known to the Japanese and Chinese long before the time of Columbus. Accounts of it were recorded in their books previous to his time. They called it "Fusang," and evidently, at some period, had been accustomed to make voyages to some part of the American coast. But neither the Malays, the Chinese, nor the

* See Appendix C.

Japanese came here as civilizers, for there is no trace of either of those peoples in the old ruins, in the ancient language of the country, or in any thing we know of the people whom these American ruins represent.

THE PHŒNICIAN THEORY.

Some of the more intelligent investigators have maintained, with no little confidence, that this ancient American civilization came originally from the Phœnicians. Among those who use reason in their inquiries sufficiently to be incapable of accepting the absurdities of monkish fancy, this hypothesis has found more favor than any other. Wherever inquiry begins by assuming that the original civilizers came from some other part of the world, it seems more reasonable than any other, for more can be said to give it the appearance of probability.

The people known to us as Phœnicians were pre-eminent as the colonizing navigators of antiquity. They were an enlightened and enterprising maritime people, whose commerce traversed every known sea, and extended its operations beyond the "Pillars of Hercules" into the "great exterior ocean." The early Greeks called them Ethiopians (not meaning either black men or Africans), and said they went every where, establishing their colonies and their commerce in all the coast regions, "from the extreme east to the extreme west." But the great ages of this people are in the distant past, far beyond the beginning of what we call history. History has knowledge only of a few of their later communities, the Sabeans of Southern Arabia, the Phœnicians (meaning chiefly the Tyrians), and the Carthaginians. What a change there would be in the prevalent conceptions of the past if we could have a complete record of this race from the beginning of its development!

It is not difficult to believe that communities of the Phœnician or Ethiopian race were established all around the Mediterranean, and even beyond the Strait of Gibraltar, in ages quite as old as Egypt or Chaldea, and that they had communication with America before Tyre or Sidon was built. Why did the ancients say so much of a "great Saturnian continent" beyond the Atlantic if nobody in the pre-historic ages had ever seen that continent? It was there, as they said and as we know; but whence came their knowledge of it, and such knowledge as led them to describe it as "larger than Asia (meaning Asia Minor), Europe, and Libya together?" This ancient belief must have been due to Phœnician or Ethiopian communication with America in earlier times, which was imperfectly recollected, or perhaps never completely revealed to other nations; and this must have taken place at a very remote period, for imperfect recollection of the great continent across the Atlantic, including what Solon heard in Egypt of Atlantis, was more ancient than the constrained voyage of that Tyrian ship of which Diodorus Siculus gives an account; and it can be seen that the early Greeks had a better knowledge even of Western Europe than those of later times. A dark age, so far as relates to geographical knowledge, set in upon the countries around the Ægean Sea and on the coast of Asia Minor after the independence and enterprise of Tyre and the other Phœnician cities were destroyed by the Assyrians, toward the close of the ninth century before Christ, which was disturbed some four hundred and fifty or five hundred years later by the conquests of Alexander the Great.

The known enterprise of the Phœnician race, and this ancient knowledge of America, so variously expressed, strongly encourage the hypothesis that the people called Phœnicians came to this continent, established colonies in the region where ruined cities are found, and filled it with civilized life. It is argued that they made voyages on the "great exterior ocean," and that such navigators must have crossed the Atlantic; and it is added that symbolic devices similar to those of the Phœnicians are found in the American ruins, and that an old tradition of the native Mexicans and Central Americans described the first civilizers as "bearded white men," who "came from the East in ships." Therefore, it is urged, the people described in the native books and traditions as "Colhuas" must have been Phœnicians.

But if it were true that the civilization found in Mexico and Central America came from people of the Phœnician race, it would be true also that they built in America as they never built any where else, that they established a language here radically unlike their own, and that they used a style of writing totally different from that which they carried into every other region occupied by their colonies. All the forms of alphabetical writing used at present in Europe and Southwestern Asia came directly or indirectly from that anciently invented by the race to which the Phœnicians belonged, and they have traces of a common relationship which can easily be detected. Now the writing of the inscriptions at Palenque, Copan, and elsewhere in the ruins has no more relatedness to the Phœnician than to the Chinese writing. It has not a single characteristic that can be called Phœnician any more than the language of the inscriptions or the style of architecture with which it is associated; therefore we can not reasonably suppose this American civilization was originated by people of the Phœnician race, whatever may be thought relative to the supposed ancient communication between the two continents and its probable influence on civilized communities already existing here.

THE "ATLANTIC" THEORY.

I have already stated in general terms the hypothesis advanced by Brasseur de Bourbourg and some other writers. This may be called the "Atlantic" theory, for it attributes the civilization of Ancient America to the Atlantides or Atlantic race, who occupied the lost "island of Atlantis." Brasseur de Bourbourg has studied the monuments, writings, and traditions left by this civilization more carefully and thoroughly than any other man living. He has fancies which may be safely rejected, and he has theories which, doubtless, will always lack confirmation; but he has much, also, which demands respectful consideration. There is a great deal in his books to provoke criticism; those well acquainted with the antiquities and ancient speech of Egypt may reasonably give way to a smile of incredulity while reading what he says in support of the notion that the great civilization of Egypt also came originally from this Atlantic race. Nevertheless, his volumes are important, because they furnish materials which others can use more carefully, and because he has learned to decipher some of the Central American writings and brought to view certain paths of inquiry which others may pursue with a more rigid method.

As already stated, his Atlantic theory of the old American civilization is, that it was originated on this continent, but on a portion of the continent which is now below the waters of the Atlantic Ocean. It supposes the continent extended, anciently, from New Granada, Central America, and Mexico in a long, irregular peninsula, so far across the Atlantic that the Canary, Madeira, and Azores or Western Islands may be remains of this portion of it. High mountains stood where we now find the West India islands. Beyond these, toward Africa and Europe, was a great extent of fertile and beautiful land, and here arose the first civilization of mankind, which flourished many ages, until at length this extended portion of the continent was ingulfed by a tremendous convulsion of nature, or by a succession of such convulsions which made the ruin complete. After the cataclysm, a part of the Atlantic people who escaped destruction settled in Central America, where perhaps their civilization had been previously introduced. The reasons urged in support of this hypothesis make it seem plausible, if not probable, to imaginative minds.

In the first place, Brasseur de Bourbourg claims that there is in the old Central American books a constant tradition of an immense catastrophe of the character supposed; that this tradition existed every where among the people when they first became known to Europeans; and that recollections of the catastrophe were preserved in some of their festivals, especially in one celebrated in the month of *Izcalli*, which was instituted to commemorate this frightful destruction of land and people, and in which "princes and people humbled themselves before the divinity, and besought Him to withhold a return of such terrible calamities." This tradition affirms that a part of the continent extending into the Atlantic was destroyed in the manner supposed, and appears to indicate that the destruction was accomplished by a succession of frightful convulsions. Three are constantly mentioned, and sometimes there is mention of one or two others. "The land was shaken by frightful earthquakes, and the waves of the sea combined with volcanic fires to overwhelm and ingulf it." Each convulsion swept away portions of the land, until the whole disappeared, leaving the line of the coast as it is now. Most of the inhabitants, overtaken amid their regular employments, were destroyed; but some escaped in ships, and some fled for safety to the summits of high mountains, or to portions of the land which, for the time, escaped immediate destruction. Quotations are made from the old books in which this tradition is recorded which appear to verify his report of what is found in them. To criticise intelligently his interpretation of their significance, one needs to have a knowledge of those books and traditions equal at least to his own.

In the second place, he appeals to the story of Atlantis, preserved in the annals of Egypt, and related to Solon by the priests of Sais. It is stated in Plutarch's life of Solon that while in Egypt "he conferred with the priests of Psenophis, Sonchis, Heliopolis, and Sais, and learned from them the story of Atlantis." Brasseur de Bourbourg cites Cousin's translation of Plato's record of this story as follows:

"Among the great deeds of Athens, of which recollection is preserved in our books, there is one which should be placed above all others. Our books tell that the Athenians destroyed an army which came across the Atlantic Sea, and insolently invaded Europe and Asia; for this sea was then navigable, and beyond the strait where you place the Pillars of Hercules there was an island larger than Asia [Minor] and Libya combined. From this island one could pass easily to the other islands, and from these to the continent which lies around the interior sea. The sea on this side of the strait (the Mediterranean) of which we speak resembles a harbor with a narrow entrance; but there is a genuine sea, and the land which surrounds it is a veritable continent. In the island of Atlantis reigned three kings with great and marvelous power. They had under their dominion the whole of Atlantis, several other islands, and some parts of the continent. At one time their power extended into Libya, and into Europe as far as Tyrrhenia; and, uniting their whole force, they sought to destroy our countries at a blow, but their defeat stopped the invasion and gave entire independence to all the countries on this side of the Pillars of Hercules. Afterward, in one day and one fatal night, there came mighty earthquakes and inundations, which ingulfed that warlike people; Atlantis disappeared beneath the sea, and then that sea became inaccessible, so that navigation on it ceased on account of the quantity of mud which the ingulfed island left in its place."

This invasion took place many ages before Athens was known as a Greek city. It is referred to an extremely remote antiquity. The festival known as the "Lesser Panathenæa," which, as symbolic devices used in it show, commemorated this triumph over the Atlantes, is said to have been instituted by the mythical Erichthonius in the earliest times remembered by Athenian tradition. Solon had knowledge of the Atlantes before he went to Egypt, but he heard there, for the first time, this account of their "island" and of its disappearance in a frightful cataclysm. But Atlantis is mentioned by other ancient writers. An extract preserved in Proclus, taken from a work now lost, which is quoted by Boeckh in his commentary on Plato, mentions islands in the exterior sea beyond the Pillars of Hercules, and says it was known that in one of these islands "the inhabitants preserved from their ancestors a remembrance of Atlantis, an extremely large island, which for a long time held dominion over all the islands of the Atlantic Ocean."

Brasseur de Bourbourg claims that these traditions, on both sides of the Atlantic, mean the same thing. The "island of Atlantis," larger than Libya and Asia Minor together, was the extended portion of the American continent. These concurring traditions can not be devoid of historical significance. The constant references by ancient Greek writers to the Atlantes, who are always placed at the extremity of Europe and Africa, on the ocean which bears their name, may reasonably be regarded as vague and faded recollections of such a history connected with that ocean as that implied by what was said of their island in the annals of Egypt. In support of his view of what is meant by the traditions, he adds this philological argument:

"The words *Atlas* and *Atlantic* have no satisfactory etymology in any language known to Europe. They are not Greek, and can not be referred to any known language of the Old World. But in the Nahuatl language we find immediately the radical *a*, *atl*, which signifies water, war, and the top of the head. (Molina, *Vocab. en lengua mexicana y castellana*, etc.) From this comes a series of words, such as *atlan*, on the border of or amid the water, from which we have the adjective *Atlantic*. We have also atlaça, to combat or be in agony; it means likewise to hurl or dart from the water, and in the preterit makes *atlaz*. A city named *Atlan* existed when the continent was discovered by Columbus, at the entrance of the Gulf of Uraba, in Darien, with a good harbor; it is now reduced to an unimportant pueblo named *Acla*."

In the third place, he quotes opinions expressed without any regard whatever to his theory to show that scientific men who have considered the question believe that there was formerly a great extension of the land into the Atlantic in the manner supposed. The first quotation is from Moreau de Saint-Mery's "Description topographique et politique de la Partie Espagnole a l'Isle de Saint-Domingue," published in 1796, as follows:

"There are those who, in examining the map of America, do not confine themselves to thinking with the French Pliny that the innumerable islands situated from the mouth of the Orinoco to the Bahama Channel (islands which include several *Grenadins* not always visible in very high tides or great agitations of the sea) should be considered as summits of vast mountains whose bases and sides are covered with water, but who go farther, and suppose these islands to be the tops of the most elevated of a chain of mountains which crowned a portion of the continent whose submersion has produced the Gulf of Mexico. But to sustain this opinion it must be added that another vast surface of land which united the islands of this archipelago to the continent, from Yucatan to the mouth of the Orinoco, was submerged in the same way, and also a third surface which connected them with the peninsula of Florida and with whatever land may have constituted the northern termination; for we can not imagine that these mountains whose summits appear above water stood on the terminating line of the continent."

He quotes, also, another authority which "can not be suspected," namely, M. Charles Martins, who said, in the *Revue des Deux Mondes* for March 1, 1867, "Now, hydrography, geology, and botany agree in teaching us that the Azores, the Canaries, and Madeira are the remains of a great continent which formerly united Europe to North America." He could have added other quotations in the same strain. Those geologists who believe that "our continents have long remained in nearly the same relative position" would probably give the supposed change a much greater antiquity than Brasseur de Bourbourg would be likely to accept; and the geological "Uniformitarians" would deny with emphasis that so great a change in the shape of a continent was ever effected by such means, or with such rapidity as he supposes. But the latest and most advanced school of geological speculation does not exclude "Catastrophism," and, therefore, will not deny the possibility of sudden and great changes by this method.

Doubtless the antiquity of the human race is much greater than is usually assumed by those whose views of the past are still regulated by mediæval systems of chronology. Archæology and linguistic science, not to speak here of geology, make it certain that the period between the beginning of the human race and the birth of Christ would be more accurately stated if the centuries counted in the longest estimate of the rabbinical chronologies should be changed to millenniums. And they present also another fact, namely, that the antiquity of civilization is very great, and suggest that in remote ages it may have existed, with important developments, in regions of the earth now described as barbarous, and even, as Brasseur de Bourbourg supposes, on ancient continents or portions of continents now out of sight below the surface of the oceans. The representation of some speculators that the condition of the human race since its first appearance on earth has been a condition of universal and hopeless savagery down to a comparatively modern date, is an assumption merely, an unwarranted assumption used in support of an unproved and unprovable theory of man's origin. Its use in the name of science by advocates of this theory, like the theory itself, shows that the constructive power of fancy and imagination will sometimes supersede every thing else, and substitute its ingenious constructions for legitimate conclusions, even in scientific speculation.

We may claim reasonably that Brasseur de Bourbourg's Atlantic theory is not proved, and on this ground refuse to accept it. So far as appears, it is a fanciful theory which can not be proved. No one is under obligation to attempt disproving it. It may, in some cases, win supporters by enlisting in its favor all the forces of imagination, to which it appeals with seductive plausibility. On the other hand, it will be rejected without much regard to what can be said in its favor, for it interferes with current unreasoning beliefs concerning antiquity and ancient history, and must encounter vehement contradiction from habits of thought fixed by these beliefs. True, some of the stock views of antiquity, by which it will be earnestly opposed, are themselves far more destitute of foundation in either fact or reason; but this will make no difference, as the habit of never allowing them to be subjected to the searching power of reason does not permit such persons either to believe or deny any thing connected with this topic in a reasonable manner.

Some of the uses made of this theory can not endure criticism. For instance, when he makes it the basis of an assumption that all the civilization of the Old World went originally from America, and claims particularly that the supposed "Atlantic race" created Egypt, he goes quite beyond reach of the considerations used to give his hypothesis a certain air of probability. It may be, as he says, that for every pyramid in Egypt there are a thousand in Mexico and Central America, but the ruins in Egypt and those in America have nothing in common. The two countries were entirely different in their language, in their styles of architecture, in their written characters, and in the physical characteristics of their earliest people, as they are seen sculptured or painted on the monuments. An Egyptian pyramid is no more the same thing as a Mexican pyramid than a Chinese pagoda is the same thing as an English light-house. It was not made in the same way, nor for the same uses. The ruined monuments show, in generals and in particulars, that the original civilizers in America were profoundly different from the ancient Egyptians. The two peoples can not explain each other.

This, however, does not require us to assert positively that the Central American "Colhuas" and the legendary Atlantes could not possibly have been the same people, or people of the same race. Room may be left for any amount of conjecture not inconsistent with known facts, without making it necessary to accept a theory of the origin of the old Mexican race which at present can neither be proved nor disproved.

IT WAS AN ORIGINAL CIVILIZATION.

It has been said, very justly, by one explorer of the Mexican and Central American ruins, that "the American monuments are different from those of any other known people, of a new order, and entirely and absolutely anomalous; they stand alone." The more we study them, the more we find it necessary to believe that the civilization they represent was originated in America, and probably in the region where they are found. It did not come from the Old World; it was the work of some remarkably gifted branch of the race found on the southern part of this continent when it was discovered in 1492. Undoubtedly it was very old. Its original beginning may have been as old as Egypt, or even farther back in the past than the ages to which Atlantis must be referred; and it may have been later than the beginning of Egypt. Who can certainly tell its age? Whether earlier or later, it was original.

Its constructions seem to have been a refined and artistic development of a style of building different from that of any other people, which began with ruder forms, but in all the periods of its history preserved the same general conception. They show us the idea of the Mound-Builders wrought out in stone and embellished by art. The decorations, and the writing also, are wholly original. There is no imitation of the work of any people ever known in Asia, Africa, or Europe. It appears evident that the method of building seen in the great ruins began with the ruder forms of mound-work, and became what we find it by gradual development, as the advancing civilization supplied new ideas and gave higher skill. But the culture and the work were wholly original, wholly American.

The civilized life of the ancient Mexicans and Central Americans may have had its original beginning somewhere in South America, for they seem more closely related to the ancient South Americans than to the wild Indians north of the Mexican border; but the peculiar development of it represented by the ruins must have begun in the region where they are found. I find myself more and more inclined to the opinion that the aboriginal South Americans are the oldest people on this continent; that they are distinct in race; and that the wild Indians of the North came originally from Asia, where the race to which they belong seems still represented by the Koraks and Chookchees found in that part of Asia which extends to Behring's Strait.

If, as there is reason to believe, the countries on the Mediterranean had communication with America in very ancient times, they found here a civilization already developed, and contributed nothing to change its style of building and decorating cities. They may have influenced it in other respects; for, if such communication was opened across the Atlantic, it was probably continued for a long time, and its interruption may or may not be due, as Brasseur de Bourbourg supposes, to the cataclysm which ingulfed Atlantis. Religious symbols are found in the American ruins which remind us of those of the Phœnicians, such as figures of the serpent, which appear constantly, and the cross, supposed by some to represent the mounting of the magnetic needle, which was among the emblems peculiar to the goddess Astarte. A figure appears occasionally in the sculptures, in which some have sought to recognize Astarte, one at Palenque being described as follows: "It is a female figure moulded in stucco, holding a child on her left arm and hand, just as Astarte appears on the Sidonian medals." I find it impossible to see that this figure has any resemblance whatever to the Phœnician goddess. They are not alike either in dress, posture, or expression. Dupaix describes it correctly in saying it represents a person apparently "absorbed in devotion" — a worshiper, and not a goddess. Moreover, Astarte usually appears on the medals standing on the forward deck of a vessel, holding a cross with one hand, and pointing forward with the other. And, finally, this figure seems to represent, not a woman, but a priest. There was sun-worship in America, and the phallic ceremonies existed in some places in the time of Cortez. In Asia these ceremonies and figures of the serpent were usually associated with sun-worship. Humboldt was sure that these symbols came to America from the Old World. A more careful study of the subject might have led him to modify this belief. But, whether we adopt his explanation or some other, the traditions on both sides of the Atlantic are without meaning unless it be admitted that there was communication between the two continents in times of which we have no history.

VIII.

AMERICAN ANCIENT HISTORY.

If a consecutive history of the ancient people of Central America and Mexico were ever written, it has been lost. Probably nothing of the kind ever was written in the manner which we call history, although there must have been regular annals of some kind. The ruins show that they had the art of writing, and that, at the south, this art was more developed, more like a phonetic system of writing than that found in use among the Aztecs. The inscriptions of Palenque, and the characters used in some of the manuscript books that have been preserved, are not the same as the "Mexican Picture Writing." It is known that books or manuscript writings were abundant among them in the ages previous to the Aztec period. They had an accurate measure of the solar year and a system of chronology, and many of their writings were historical. Among the Mayas, and in other communities of the same family, writing was largely used in the time of the Spaniards. It was common also among the Aztecs, but they used "picture writing." Las Casas wrote on this point as follows:

"It should be known that in all the commonwealths of these countries, in the kingdoms of New Spain and elsewhere, among other professions duly filled by suitable persons was that of chronicler and historian. These chroniclers had knowledge of the origin of the kingdoms, and of whatever related to religion and the gods, as well as to the founders of towns and cities. They recorded the history of kings, and of the modes of their election and succession; of their labors, actions, wars, and memorable deeds, good and bad; of the virtuous men or heroes of former days, their great deeds, the wars they had waged, and how they had distinguished themselves; who had been the earliest settlers, what had been their ancient customs, their triumphs, and defeats. They knew, in fact, whatever pertained to history, and were able to give an account of all past events. * * * These chroniclers had likewise to calculate the days, months, and years; and though they had no writing like ours, they had their symbols and characters through which they understood every thing; and they had great books, which were composed with such ingenuity and art that our characters were really of no great assistance to them. Our priests have seen those books, and I myself have seen them likewise, though many were burned at the instigation of the monks, who were afraid they might impede the work of conversion."

Books such as those here described by Las Casas must have contained important historical information. The older books, belonging to the ages of Copan and Palenque, went to decay doubtless long previous to his time, in the wars and revolutions of the Toltec period, or by the wear of time. The later books, not otherwise lost, were destroyed by Aztec and Spanish vandalism.

According to tradition, and the testimony of writings still in existence when the Spaniards went there, the Aztec or Mexican sovereign Ytzcoatl destroyed many of the old Toltec books. His aim was probably to exterminate among the people all memory of the previous times. Such things have been done with similar motives, as we know, in other countries, by successful usurpers and conquerors. We learn from Spanish writers that a still greater destruction of the old books was effected by the more ignorant and fanatical of the Spanish priests who were established in the country as missionaries after the Conquest. This is stated by Las Casas, himself one of the missionaries. Besides the many smaller bonfires of this fanaticism, there is record of a great conflagration, under the auspices of Bishop Zumarraga, in which a vast collection of these old writings was consumed. As the writing was all on paper (which had long been used in the country), the burning was easily accomplished.

THE OLD BOOKS NOT ALL LOST.

The Franciscan and Dominican fanatics, whose learning and religion consisted of ignorance and bigotry, hoped to exterminate among the people all recollection of their former history, ideas, and religious customs. A few of the books, however, escaped; none, indeed, that were very old, for it does not appear that any of the manuscripts rescued from destruction were written or copied earlier than the age which closed the Aztec domination. None of the great books of annals described by Las Casas are among them, but they relate to the ancient times, and most of them are copies or reproductions of much older books.

Among these destroying Spanish ecclesiastics, there was here and there one who quietly secured some of the manuscripts, or copies of them. These were kept from the flames. Others were secreted by the people; and subsequently, in years after the conquest was completed,

Fig. 48.—Inscriptions carved on Stone.

some of the more intelligent churchmen wrote histories of the country, or portions of it, which were preserved in manuscript. Sahagun wrote such a history, which shows that he had studied the traditions and some of the old books; this work is printed in the great collection of Lord Kingsborough. Diego de Landa, first bishop of Yucatan, wrote a history of the Mayas and their country, which was preserved in manuscript at Madrid in the library of the Royal Academy of History. It is one of the most important works on the country written by a Spaniard, because it contains a description and explanation of the phonetic alphabet of the Mayas. Landa's manuscript seems to have lain neglected in the library, for little or nothing was heard of it until it was discovered and studied by Brasseur de Bourbourg, who, by means of it, has deciphered some of the old American writings. He says "the alphabet and signs explained by Landa have been to me a Rosetta stone." Figure 49 represents a specimen of the inscriptions as carved upon stone. Figure 50 gives them as they appear in manuscript.

Fig. 50.—Manuscript Writing.

An extensive and important manuscript work, written two hundred years ago by Francisco Ximenes, an ecclesiastic, is preserved in Guatemala. He, being drawn to inquiries concerning the antiquities and ancient history of the country, was able to get possession of several of the old books, one of them being that known as "Popol-Vuh." His manuscript, arranged in four great volumes (one of which, it is said, has disappeared), contains valuable information in regard to the ancient history and traditions of Guatemala. One of the volumes has a copy of the "Popol-Vuh" in the native tongue, and another has a Spanish translation of the work. He left also a manuscript Dictionary of the principal Guatemalan dialects (which belong to the Maya family), entitled "Tesoro de las Lenguas Quiché, Cakchiquel, y Tzutohil." Probably other manuscripts of the same character exist at Madrid and in Central America which are not yet known to those who can understand their importance.

As already stated, none of the great books of annals have been discovered, but some of the old American manuscripts now preserved in several of the libraries and private collections of Europe are important. Three are specified as particularly valuable to students of American antiquity: that called the "Codex Chimalpopoca," an old Toltec book, written in the Toltec language; one now entitled the "Codex Cakchiquel;" and the "Popol-Vuh." The latter, written in the Quiché dialect, was translated into Spanish two hundred years ago by Ximenes, but his translation remained in Guatemala unprinted and quite unknown until it was discovered in our time. Brassour de Bourbourg, who is master of the Quiché language, and to whom we are indebted for most that is known of the manuscripts of Ximenes, thought this Spanish translation very imperfect; therefore he has translated the work into French.

The "Popol-Vuh" was written in 1558 as an abridged reproduction of a very ancient Quiché book which contained an account of the history, traditions, religion, and cosmogony of the Quichés. The first part of it is devoted to the cosmogony and traditional lore; the rest gives an account of the Quichés, who, at the time of the Conquest, were the dominant people in the Central American regions south of the great forest. If the history were consecutive and clear, it would not take us back into the past more than three or four centuries beyond 1558, for the Quiché domination was probably not much older than that of the Aztecs. But the history is not clear. Putting aside the mythical and legendary portion of it which relates to origins and migrations, we can see that it extends over some fourteen generations, which may indicate that Quiché became an independent and ruling power about 1200 A.D.

For those who study the book it is full of interest. It shows us their conceptions of the Supreme Being and his relation to the world; it enables us to see what they admired in character as virtue, heroism, nobleness, and beauty; it discloses their mythology and their notions of religious worship; in a word, it bears witness to the fact that the various families of mankind are all of "one blood," so far, at least, as to be precisely alike in nature.

The cosmogony and mythical lore of the Quichés seem to have their root in the beliefs and facts of a time far more ancient than the national beginning of this people. In assuming the form in which we find them, they must have passed through several phases of growth, which

I

changed their appearance and obscured their meaning. Manifestly the history of the country did not begin with the Quichés. The account of the creation, with every thing else in this cosmogony and mythology, is original, like the civilization to which they belong.

According to the "Popol-Vuh," the world had a beginning. There was a time when it did not exist. Only "Heaven" existed, below which all space was an empty, silent, unchanging solitude. Nothing existed there, neither man, nor animal, nor earth, nor tree. Then appeared a vast expanse of water on which divine beings moved in brightness. "They said 'earth!' and instantly the earth was created. It came into being like a vapor; mountains rose above the waters like lobsters and were made. Thus was the earth created by the Heart of Heaven." Next came the creation of animals; but the gods were disappointed because the animals could neither tell their names nor worship the Heart of Heaven.

Therefore it was resolved that man should be created. First, man was made of earth, but his flesh had no cohesion; he was inert, could not turn his head, and had no mind, although he could speak; therefore he was consumed in the water. Next, men were made of wood, and these multiplied, but they had neither heart nor intellect, and could not worship, and so they withered up and disappeared in the waters. A third attempt followed: man was made of a tree called tzité, and woman of the pith of a reed; but these failed to think, speak, or worship, and were destroyed, all save a remnant which still exists as a race of small monkeys found in forests.

A fourth attempt to create the human race was successful, but the circumstances attending this creation are veiled in mystery. It took place before the beginning of dawn, when neither sun nor moon had risen, and was a wonder-work of the Heart of Heaven. Four men were created, and they could reason, speak, and see in such a manner as to know all things at once. They worshiped the Creator with thanks for existence, but the gods, dismayed and scared, breathed clouds on their eyes to limit their vision, and cause them to be men and not gods. Afterward, while the four men were asleep, the gods made for them beautiful wives, and from these came all the tribes and families of the earth.

No account of the rescued fragments of this old literature of Ancient America should omit giving due credit to Chevalier Boturini, the Milanese, who went from Italy to America in 1735 as an agent of the Countess Santibañey, who claimed to be a descendant of Montezuma. He, too, was a devotee, and believed that St. Thomas preached the Gospel in America; but he had antiquarian tastes, and was sufficiently intelligent to understand the importance of the old manuscripts which had furnished so much fuel for the bonfires of fanaticism. During the eight years of his residence in Mexico and Central America he hunted diligently for those still in existence, and made a considerable collection, including in it some of the Mexican "picture writings." But when about to leave, he was despoiled of his treasure and flung into prison by the Spanish viceroy. He finally left the country with a portion of them, but was captured by an English cruiser and again despoiled. The manuscripts left in Mexico were finally sold at auction while Humboldt was there; he secured a portion of them. Another portion was brought to France about 1830 by M. Aubin, who made important additions to it. M. Aubin himself spent years searching for remains of the old writings, and he has now, it is supposed, the most valuable collection in Europe.

It is likely that most of the recovered books may be translated by those who can bring to the work habits of patient study and a thorough knowledge of the native dialects. Dictionaries of these dialects, as they were spoken at the time of the Conquest, were prepared by some of the Spanish priests, and other facilities are not wanting. It is surprising, however, that no one has translated the "Codex Chimalpopoca" (which seems the most important) if the language in which it is written is in fact sufficiently modern to be managed as easily as that of "Popol Vuh." It must be translatable, for its general tenor is known, and passages of it are quoted. Brasseur de Bourbourg states that he has undertaken a translation. But who will translate the inscriptions at Copan and Palenque? Is the language in which they were written an old form of speech, from which the dialects of the Maya family, or a portion of them, were derived? They have not been translated. No one has found a clew to their meaning. The characters are understood, but they appear to show an older form of the language, which at present can not be deciphered. Brasseur de Bourbourg's "Rosetta Stone," discovered in Landa's manuscript, will not serve him here. Another more potent must be found before these old inscriptions can be made to give up their secrets.*

THE ANCIENT HISTORY SKETCHED.

It is impossible to know what was contained in the books of annals written by the official chroniclers of these ancient American countries, for these books are lost. They existed at the time of the Conquest; some of them were seen and described by Las Casas; but, so far as is known, not one of these books of regular anuals, such as he described, has escaped destruction; therefore it is impossible to know any thing certainly of their character as histories.

The books preserved furnish little more than vague outlines of the past, with obscure views of distinct periods in the history, created by successive dominations of different peoples or different branches of the same people. What they enable us to know of the old history resembles what is known of the early times of the Greeks, who had no ancient histories excepting such as were furnished by their "poets of the cycle." In one case we are told of Pelasgians, Leleges, Cadmeans, Argives, and Eolians very much as in the other we are told of Colhuas, Chichimeca, Qninames, and Nahuas.

But the outline is not wholly dark; it does not exclude the possibility of a reasonable attempt at hypothesis. When Cortez entered Mexico, the Aztecs, Montezuma's people, had been in power more than two centuries.

* See Appendix D.

Most of the ancient history, of which something is said in these books, relates to ages previous to their time, and chiefly to their predecessors, the Toltecs. According to these writings, the country where the ruins are found was occupied in successive periods by three distinct peoples, the Chichimecs, the Colhuas, and the Toltecs or Nahuas. The Toltecs are said to have come into the country about a thousand years before the Christian era. Their supremacy appears to have ceased, and left the country broken up into small states, two or three centuries before the Aztecs appeared. They were preceded by the Colhuas, by whom this old civilization was originated and developed. The most ancient people, those found in the country by the Colhuas, are called Chichimecs. They are described as a barbarous people who lived by hunting and fishing, and had neither towns nor agriculture. This term Chichimecs appears to have been a generic appellation for all uncivilized aborigines. Brasseur de Bourbourg says, "Under the generic name Chichimecs, which has much embarrassed some writers, the Mexican traditions include the whole aboriginal population of the New World, and especially the people by whom it was first occupied at the beginning of time."

Some of the traditions state that the Colhuas came from the east in ships. Sahagun mentions that a tradition to this effect was current in Yucatan. The precise value of these traditional reports is uncertain; but, if accepted as vague historical recollections, they could be explained by supposing the civilized people called Colhuas came from South America through the Caribbean

Sea, and landed in Yucatan and Tabasco. They are uniformly described as the people who first established civilization and built great cities. They taught the Chichimecs to cook their food, cultivate the earth, and adopt the ways of civilized life; and the Chichimecs civilized by their influence are sometimes called Quinames.

The Colhuas are connected with vague references to a long and important period in the history previous to the Toltec ages. They seem to have been, in some respects, more advanced in civilization than the Toltecs. What is said of events in their history relates chiefly to their great city called Xibalba, the capital of an important kingdom to which this name was given. The Toltecs, in alliance with the uncivilized Chichimecs of the mountains, subjugated this city and kingdom, and thus brought to a close the period which may be termed Colhuan. This kingdom appears to have included Guatemala, Yucatan, Tabasco, Tehuantepec, Chiapa, Honduras, and other districts in Central America; and it may have included all Southern Mexico, for places north of the Tampico River are mentioned as being within its limits when the Toltecs came into the country. Some of the principal seats of the Colhuan civilization were in the region now covered by the great forest. Some investigators have sought to identify the city of Xibalba with the ruined city known to us as Palenque. Brasseur de Bourbourg says: "Palenque appears to have been the same city to which the books give the name of Xibalba;" but this is nothing but conjecture. We may as reasonably suppose Copan, Quirigua, or some other old ruin, to have been Xibalba.

Those who attempt to believe this old American civilization was brought across the Atlantic by the Phœnicians in very remote times, assume, against the plain testimony of the monuments, that the Colhuas came to America from some country on the Mediterranean. They may have come from some other part of this continent. In my judgment, it is not improbable that they came by sea from South America. Brasseur de Bourbourg would say they were people of the Atlantic race, who, having escaped destruction by the cataclysm, found their way to Yucatan and Tabasco. But there is little beside conjecture to support any theory of their origin. We have only the fact that, according to the old books and traditions of the country, they occupied that region at a remote period, and originated the civilization whose monuments are found there. Tradition places their first settlements on the Gulf coast in Tabasco, between Tehuantepec and Yucatan. It is inferred that the Mayas, Tzendals, Quichés, and some other communities of the old race, were descendants of the Colhuas, their speech being more highly developed than that of any native community not connected with this family, and their written characters having a close resemblance to those of the oldest inscriptions.

THE TOLTECS OUR MOUND-BUILDERS.

As the remains of the Mound-Builders show clearly that they had commercial intercourse with the Mexican and Central American countries, and as it seems probable that they had otherwise a very close relation to the

people of those countries, it would be surprising to find
no mention of their country in the old books and traditions of the Central Americans and Mexicans. If we
could have the lost books, especially those of the more
ancient time, and learn to read them, it might be possible to know something of the origin and history of the
Mound-Builders. It is believed that distinct reference
to their country has been found in the books still in existence, and there appears to be reason for this belief.
Brasseur de Bourbourg, one of the few investigators who
have explored them, says:

"Previous to the history of the Toltec domination in
Mexico, we notice in the annals of the country two facts
of great importance, but equally obscure in their details:
first, the tradition concerning the landing of a foreign
race, conducted by an illustrious personage, who came
from an eastern country; and, second, the existence of
an ancient empire known as Huehue-Tlapalan, from
which the Toltecs or Nahuas came to Mexico, in conse-
quence of a revolution or invasion, and from which they
had a long and toilsome migration to the Aztec plateau."

He believes that Huehue-Tlapalan was the country of
the Mound-Builders in the Mississippi and Ohio Valleys.
According to the native books he has examined, it was
somewhere at a distance in the northeast; and it is constantly said that some of the Toltecs came by land and
some by sea. Sahagun learned from the old books and
traditions, and stated in the introduction to the first
book of his history, that the Toltecs came from that distant northeastern country; and he mentions a company

that came by sea, settled near the Tampico River, and built a town called Panuco. Brasseur de Bourbourg finds that an account of this or another company was preserved at Xilanco, an ancient city situated on the point of an island between Lake Terminos and the sea, and famous for its commerce, wealth, and intelligence. The company described in this account came from the northeast in the same way, it is said, to the Tampico River, and landed at Panuco. It consisted of twenty chiefs and a numerous company of people. Torquemada found a record which describes them as people of fine appearance. They went forward into the country and were well received. He says they were industrious, orderly, and intelligent, and that they worked metals, and were skillful artists and lapidaries. All the accounts say the Toltecs came at different times, by land and sea, mostly in small companies, and always from the northeast. This can be explained only by supposing they came by sea from the mouth of the Mississippi River or from the Gulf coast near it, and by land through Texas. But the country from which they came was invariably Huehue-Tlapalan.

Cabrera says Huehue-Tlapalan was the ancient country of the Toltecs. Its simple name was Tlapalan, but they called it Huehue, old, to distinguish it from three other Tlapalans which they founded in the districts of their new kingdom. Torquemada says the same. We are not authorized to reject a fact so distinctly stated and so constantly reported in the old books. The most we can do against it with any show of reason is to receive it with doubt. Therefore it seems not improbable that the "Old Tlapalan" of Central American tradition was the country of our Mound-Builders.

Another circumstance mentioned is not without significance. It is said, in connection with this account of the Toltec migration, that Huehue-Tlapalan was successfully invaded by Chichimecs, meaning barbarous aboriginal tribes, who were united under one great leader. Here is one statement (a little condensed) touching this point: "There was a terrible struggle, but, after about thirteen years, the Toltecs, no longer able to resist successfully, were obliged to abandon their country to escape complete subjugation. Two chiefs guided the march of the emigrating nation. At length they reached a region near the sea named 'Tlapalan-Conco,' where they remained several years. But they finally undertook another migration and reached Mexico, where they built a town called 'Tollanzinco,' and later the city of Tullan, which became the seat of their government."

This is substantially what is told of the defeat and migrations of the Toltecs. The history of Ixtlilxochitl adds doubtful modifications and particulars not found in the "Codex Chimalpopoca." (See Quatre Lettres, etc.) This Chichimec invasion of Huehue-Tlapalan is placed at a period which, in the chronology of the native books, was long previous to the Christian era, and is mentioned to explain the beginning of the Toltec movement toward Mexico; but the account of it is obscure.

To find a system of chronology in these old books is not surprising when we consider that even the Aztecs of

Montezuma's time knew enough of astronomy to have a correct measure of the year. The Aztecs adopted the methods of astronomy and chronology which were used by their predecessors. They divided the year into eighteen months of twenty days each; but, as this gave the year only three hundred and sixty days, five supplementary days were added to each year, and a sixth day to every fourth year. The bissextile is known to have been used by the Mayas, Tzendals, and Quichés, and it was probably common.

We can not reasonably refuse to give some attention to their chronology, even while doubting its value as a means of fixing dates and measuring historical periods. Its method was to count by equal periods of years, as we count by centuries, and their chronology presents a series of periods which carries back their history to a very remote time in the past. Brasseur de Bourbourg says: "In the histories written in the Nahuatl language, the oldest certain date is nine hundred and fifty-five years before Christ." This, he means, is the oldest date in the history of the Nahuas or Toltecs which has been accurately determined. The calculation by which it is found is quoted from the later portion of the "Codex Chimalpopoca" as follows: "Six times 400 years plus 113 years" previous to the year 1558 A.D. This is given as the date of a division of the land by the Nahuas. The division was made 2513 years previous to 1558 A.D., or in 955 B.C. If this date could be accepted as authentic, it would follow that the Nahuas or Toltecs left Huehue-Tlapalan more than a thousand years previous to the

Christian era, for they dwelt a long time in the country of Xibalba as peaceable settlers before they organized the civil war which raised them to power.

SOME CONFIRMATION OF THIS HISTORY.

That the ancient history of the country was something like what is reported in the old writings seems not improbable when we consider the condition in which the native population was found three hundred and fifty years ago. This shows that Mexico and Central America had been subjected to disrupting political changes caused by violent transfers of supreme influence from one people to another several times in the course of a long history. Such a history is indicated by the monuments, and its traces were noticeable in peculiarities of the native inhabitants of the various districts at the time of the Spanish Conquest. They are still manifest to travelers who study the existing representatives of the old race and the old dialects sufficiently to find them. There were several distinct families or groups of language, and, in many cases, the people represented by each family of dialects were in a state of separation or disruption. To a considerable extent they existed in fragmentary communities, sometimes widely separated.

The most important group of related dialects was that which included the speech of the Mayas, Quichés, and Tzendals, which, it is supposed, represented the language of the original civilizers, the Colhuas. Dialects of this family are found on both sides of the great forest. There were other dialects supposed to indicate Toltec communities; and there were communities south of Mexico, in Nicaragua, and even farther south, which used the Aztec speech. Very likely all these differing groups of language came originally from the same source, and really represent a single race, but comparative philology has not yet reported on them. Mention is made of another people, called Waiknas or Caribs, and conjecture sees in them remains of the aboriginal barbarians termed Chichimecs. They dwelt chiefly in the "dense, dank forests" found growing on the low alluvion of the Atlantic coast. So far as is known, their speech had no affinity with that of any other native community. People of this race constitute a chief element in the mixed population of the "Mosquito Coast," known as Moscos.

In Yucatan the old inhabitants were Mayas, and people using dialects related to theirs were numerous in Tabasco, Chiapa, Guatemala, and the neighboring districts, while all around the country were scattered communities supposed to be of Toltec origin, as their speech could not be classed with these dialects nor with that of the Aztecs. The most reasonable explanation of this condition of the people is that furnished by the old chronicles and traditions. The country must have been occupied, during successive periods, by different peoples, who are represented by these broken communities and unlike groups of language. When all the native writings still in existence shall have been translated, and especially when the multitude of inscriptions found in the ruins shall have been deciphered, we may be able to see in a clearer light the ruins, the people, and their history.

IX.

THE AZTEC CIVILIZATION.

If a clever gleaner of the curious and notable things in literature should write on the curiosities of historical speculation, he would be sure to take some account of "A New History of the Conquest of Mexico" published in Philadelphia in 1859. The special aim of this work is to deny utterly the civilization of the Aztecs. The author has ability, earnestness, and knowledge of what has been written on the subject; he writes with vigor, and with a charming extravagance of dogmatic assumption, which must be liked for its heartiness, while it fails to convince those who study it. This writer fully admits the significance of the old ruins, and maintains that a great civilization formerly existed in that part of the continent. This he ascribes to the Phœnicians, while he gives it an extreme antiquity, and thinks the present ruins have existed as ruins "for thousands of years," explaining these words to mean that their history "is separated by a cycle of thousands of years from the civilization of our day." In his view, the people who constructed the old cities were subjugated and destroyed, long ages since, "by inroads of northern savages," who were the only people in the country when the Spaniards arrived.

The chief business of this "New History" is to set forth these views. Under the treatment of its author, Montezuma becomes a rude Indian sachem, his kingdom a confederation of barbarous Indian tribes like that of the Iroquois, the city of Mexico a cluster of mud huts or wigwams in an everglade, its causeways rude Indian footpaths, its temples and palaces pure fictions of lying Spanish romance, and all previous histories of the Aztecs and their country extravagant inventions with a "Moorish coloring." He would have us believe that what he calls "the pretended civilization of Montezuma and his Aztecs" was a monstrous fable of the Spaniards, a "pure fabrication," encouraged by the civil authority in Spain, and supported by the censorship of the Inquisition. Therefore he undertakes to destroy "the fabric of lies," unveil those "Mexican savages" the Aztecs, and tell a "new" story of their actual character and condition.

Of course, views so preposterous do not find much favor. If the Mexicans had been nothing more than this, the experience of Cortez among them would have been like that of De Soto in his long and disastrous march through Florida, the Gulf regions, and the country on the lower Mississippi. Cortez and his men had a different fortune, because their march was among people who had towns, cities, settled communities, and the appliances and accumulations of civilized life. Doubtless some of the Spaniards exaggerated and romanced for effect in Spain, but they did not invent either the city of Mexico or the kingdom of Montezuma. We can see clearly that the Mexicans were a civilized people, that Montezuma's city of Mexico was larger than the present city, and that an important empire was substantially conquered when that city was finally subjugated and destroyed.

That the ancient city of Mexico was a great city, well built partly of timber and partly of cut stone laid in a mortar of lime, appears in all that is said of the siege, and of the dealings of Cortez with its people and their rulers. Montezuma, wishing to remove false notions of the Spaniards concerning his wealth, said to Cortez during their first interview, "The Tlascalans, I know, have told you that I am like a god, and that all about me is gold, silver, and precious stones; but you now see that I am mere flesh and blood, and that *my houses are built of lime, stone, and timber.*" Lime, stone, and timber! This was the poorest view of the old city of Mexico that could be given to those who saw it. It is not easy to understand how a denial of the Aztec civilization was possible.

THE DISCOVERY AND INVASION.

The first inhabitants of that part of the continent seen by Spaniards were Mayas from Yucatan. Columbus met them in 1502 at an island near Ruatan, off the coast of Honduras. While he was stopping at this island, these Mayas came there "in a vessel of considerable size" from a port in Yucatan, thirty leagues distant. It was a trading vessel, freighted with a variety of merchandise, and it used sails. Its cargo consisted of a variety of textile fabrics of divers colors, wearing apparel, arms, household furniture, and cacao, and the crew numbered twenty men. Columbus, who treated them very kindly, described these strangers as well clothed, intelligent, and altogether superior to any other people he had discovered in America. Adventurers hunting for prey soon began to make voyages in that direction and report what they saw. Sailing along the coast of Yucatan, they discovered cities, and "the grandeur of the buildings filled them with astonishment." On the main land and on one or two islands they saw great edifices built of stone. The seeming riches and other attractions of the country led the Spaniards to invade Yucatan, but they were defeated and driven off. At this time they gained considerable knowledge of Mexico, and persuaded themselves that immense wealth could be found there.

Finally, in March, 1519, Cortez landed near the place where Vera Cruz was afterward built, and moved on through the country toward the city of Mexico. Studying, in all the histories of the Conquest, only their incidental references to the civilized condition of the people, we can see plainly what it was. As the invaders approached Tlascala, they found "beautiful whitewashed houses" scattered over the country. The Tlascalans had towns, cities, agriculture, and markets. Cortez found among them all that was needed by his troops. His supremacy in Tlascala was easily established; and it was not difficult to induce the people to aid him cordially in his operations against Mexico, for they hated the Aztecs, by whom they had recently been subjugated. In a description of their capital, he stated that it was as large as the city of Granada, in Spain.

He went next to Cholula, where, near the great mound, was an important city, in which they saw a "great plaza." Bernal Diaz said of this city, "I well remember, when we first entered this town and looked up to the elevated white temples, how the whole place put us completely in mind of Valladolid." The "white temples" were "elevated" because they stood on high pyramidal foundations, just as they are seen in the old ruins. It is probable, however, that these were built of adobe bricks or of timber. The city very likely was much older than the Aztec empire. A Spanish officer named Ordaz ascended Mount Popocatapetl, and one thing he saw was "the Valley of Mexico, with its city, its lagunas and islands, and its scattered hamlets, a busy throng of life being every where visible."

THE CITY OF MEXICO.

At the city of Mexico Cortez had a great reception, negotiation having established the form of friendly relations between him and Montezuma. Quarters were provided in the city for the Spanish portion of his army, a vast edifice being set apart for their use which furnished ample accommodations for the whole force. The place could be entered only by causeways. They marched on a wide avenue which led through the heart of the city, beholding the size, architecture, and beauty of the Aztec capital with astonishment. This avenue was lined with some of the finest houses, built of a porous red stone dug from quarries in the neighborhood. The people gathered in crowds on the streets, on the flat roofs, in the doorways, and at the windows to witness the arrival of the Spaniards. Most of the streets were narrow, and had houses of a much less imposing character. The great streets went over numerous canals, on well-built bridges. Montezuma's palace was a low, irregular pile of stone structures extending over a large space of ground.

Among the *teocallis* of the Aztec capital the "great temple" stood foremost. It was situated in the centre of a vast inclosure, which was surrounded by a heavy wall eight feet high, built of prepared stone. This inclosure was entered by four gateways opening on the four principal streets of the city. The "temple" was a solid structure built of earth and pebbles, and faced from top to bottom with hewn stone laid in mortar. It had five stages, each receding so as to be smaller than that below it. In general outline it was a rectangular pyramid three hundred feet square at the base, with a level summit of considerable extent, on which were two towers, and two altars where "perpetual fires" were maintained. Here the religious ceremonies were conducted. The ascent was by a circular flight of steps on the outside which went four times around the structure. The water in the lagoons being salt, the city was supplied with water by means of an aqueduct which extended to Chapultepec.

Such substantially is the account given of the old city of Mexico and its great temple by every writer who saw

them before the Conquest, and all the struggles which
took place for possession of this capital had a character
that would have been impossible any where save in a
large city. In every account of the attacks on the great
temple, we can see that it was a great temple; and we
may perceive what the old city was by reading any account of the desperate and bloody battles in which the
Spaniards were driven from it, after standing a ten days'
siege in the great stone building they occupied.

THE CONQUEST.

This battle took place in the latter part of June, 1520,
several months after the friendly reception, and was occasioned by the treacherous and most atrocious proceed-
ings of the Spaniards, which drove the Mexicans to mad-
ness. Nearly a year passed before Cortez made another
attack on the Mexican capital. During this time he
found means among the Tlascalans to build a flotilla of
thirteen vessels, which were transported in pieces to Lake
Tezcuco and there put together. This would have been
impossible if he had not found in the country suitable
tools and mechanics. By means of these vessels armed
with cannon, and assisted by a great army of native al-
lies consisting of Tlascalans, Cholulans, and many others,
he took control of the lagunas, secured possession of the
causeways, and attacked the city in vain for forty-five
days, although his men several times penetrated to the
great square. He now resolved to enter by gradual ad-
vances, and destroy every thing as he went. This he
did, burning what was combustible, and tearing down

most of the edifices built of stone; nevertheless, thirty or forty days more passed before this work of destruction was complete. The inhabitants of the city were given-over to extermination.

The conquerors proceeded immediately to rebuild the city, native architects chiefly being employed to do the work. Materials for the rebuilding were taken from the ruins; probably many of the old Aztec foundations were retained, and there may now be edifices in the city of Mexico which stand on some of these foundations. Twelve acres of the great inclosure of the Aztec temple were taken for a Spanish plaza, and are still used for this purpose, while the site of the temple is occupied by a cathedral. The plaza is paved with marble. Like the rest of the great inclosure, it was paved when the Spaniards first saw it, and the paving was so perfect and so smooth that their horses were liable to slip and fall when they attempted to ride over it.

Some relics recovered from ruins of the old temple have been preserved. Among them is the great Aztec calendar which belonged to it, on which are carved hieroglyphics representing the months of the year. This calendar was found in 1790 buried in the great square. It was carved from a mass of porous basalt, and made eleven feet eight inches in diameter. It was a fixture of the Aztec temple; it is now walled into one side of the cathedral. The "stone of sacrifice," another relic of the temple, nine feet in diameter, and covered with sculptured hieroglyphics, can still be seen in the city, and in the suburbs, it is said, vestiges of the ruins of long lines of edifices can be traced. Calendars made of gold and silver were common in Mexico. Before Cortez reached the capital, Montezuma sent him two "as large as cartwheels," one representing the sun, the other the moon, both "richly carved." During the sack of the city a calendar of gold was found by a soldier in a pond of Guatemozin's garden. But these Spaniards did not go to Mexico to study Aztec astronomy, nor to collect curiosities. In their hands every article of gold was speedily transformed into coin.

In every Spanish description of the city we can see its resemblance to cities whose ruins are found farther south. If the Spaniards had invented the temple, they would not have made it unlike any thing they had ever before seen or heard of, by placing its altar on the summit of a high pyramid. This method of constructing temples is seen in the old ruins, but it was unknown to Cortez and his men until they found it in Mexico. The only reasonable or possible explanation of what they said of it is, that the temple actually existed at the Aztec capital, and that the Spaniards, being there, described what they saw. The uniform testimony of all who saw the country at that time shows that the edifices of towns and cities, wherever they went, were most commonly built of cut stone laid in mortar, or of timber, and that in the more rural districts thatch was frequently used for the roofs of dwellings. Moreover, we are told repeatedly that the Spaniards employed "Mexican masons," and found them "very expert" in the arts of building and plastering. There is no good reason to doubt that the civilized condition of the country, when the Spaniards found it, was superior to what it has been at any time since the Conquest.

WHO WERE THE AZTECS?

The Mexicans, or Aztecs, subjugated by Cortez, were themselves invaders, whose extended dominion was probably less than two hundred and fifty years old, although they had been much longer in the Valley of Mexico. There were important portions of the country, especially at the south, to which their rule had not been extended. In several districts besides those of the Mayas and the Quichés the natives still maintained independent governments. The Aztec conquest of the central region, between the Gulf of Mexico and the Pacific, was completed only a few years previous to the arrival of the Spaniards, and the conquest of this region had not been fully secured at some points, as appeared in the readiness of the Tlascalans and others to act in alliance with Cortez. But the Aztecs did not come from abroad. They belonged in the country, and seem to have been originally an obscure and somewhat rude branch of the native race.

It is very probable that the Colhuas and Nahuas or Toltecs of the old books and traditions, together with the Aztecs, were all substantially the same people. They established in the country three distinct family groups of language, it is said, but the actual significance of this difference in speech has not been clearly determined. These unlike groups of language have not been suffi-

ciently analyzed and studied to justify us in assuming
that they did not all come from the same original source,
or that there is a more radical difference between them
than between the Sclavonic, Teutonic, and Scandinavian
groups in Europe. These ancient Americans were distinct from each other at the time of the Conquest, but
not so distinct as to show much difference in their religious ideas, their mythology, their ceremonies of worship,
their methods of building, or in the general character of
their civilization.

If the Toltecs and our Mound-Builders were the same
people, they probably went from Mexico and Central
America to the Valley of the Mississippi at a very remote period, as Colhuan colonies, and after a long residence there returned so much changed in speech and in
other respects as to seem a distinct people. The Aztecs
appear to have dwelt obscurely in the south before they
rose to power. They must have been at first much less
advanced in civilization than their predecessors, but ready
to adopt the superior knowledge and methods of the
country they invaded.

THEY CAME FROM THE SOUTH.

It has sometimes been assumed that the Aztecs came
to Mexico from the north, but there is nothing to warrant this assumption, nothing to make it probable, nothing even to explain the fact that some persons have entertained it. People of the ancient Mexican and Central
American race are not found farther north than New
Mexico and Arizona, where they are known as Pueblos,

K

or Village Indians. In the old times that was a frontier region, and the Pueblos seem to represent ancient settlers who went there from the south. There was the border line between the Mexican race and the wild Indians, and the distinction between the Pueblos and the savage tribes is every way so uniform and so great that it is well-nigh impossible to believe they all belong to the same race. In fact, no people really like our wild Indians of North America have ever been found in Mexico, Central America, or South America.

Investigation has made it probable that the Mexicans or Aztecs went to the Valley of Mexico from the south. Mr. Squier says: "The hypothesis of a migration from Nicaragua and Cuscutlan to Anahuac is altogether more consonant with probabilities and with tradition than that which derives the Mexicans from the north; and it is a significant fact, that in the map of their migrations presented by Gemelli, the place of the origin of the Aztecs is designated by the sign of water (*atl* standing for Aztlan), a pyramidal temple with grades, and near these a palm-tree." Humboldt thought this indicated a southern origin.

Communities of Aztecs still exist as far south as Nicaragua and Costa Rica, with some variations in their speech, but not so great, probably, as to make them unintelligible to each other. The Spanish historian, Oviedo, called attention to the fact that an isolated community of Aztecs was found occupying the territory between Lake Nicaragua and the Pacific. They were called Niquirans, and Mr. Squier seems to have verified this fact. The result of his investigation is that the people of the district specified are Aztecs, and that, "from the comparative lateness of the separation or some other cause," their distinguishing features were easily recognized, their speech being nearly identical with the native speech heard in the Valley of Mexico. Oviedo said of them : "The Niquirans who speak the Mexican language have the same manners and appearance as the people of New Spain (Mexico)." In the neighboring districts, communities closely related to the Mayas are found, and others that appear to belong to the Toltec family. Aztecs are found still farther south, and there appear to be conclusive reasons for believing that Montezuma's people went from the south to Anahuac or Mexico.

According to the native histories as reported by Clavigero, the Aztecs began their migration northward from Aztlan about the year 1160 A.D., and founded the more important of their first settlements in the Valley of Mexico about the year 1216 A.D., a little over three hundred years previous to the Spanish invasion. Another result of investigation adds a century to this estimate. This result is reached as follows: the Mexicans stated constantly that their calendar was reformed some time after they left Aztlan, and that in the year 1519 eight cycles of fifty-two years each and thirteen years of a ninth cycle had passed since that reform was made. This carries back the beginning of their migration considerably beyond the year 1090 A.D.

Their sway seems to have been confined for a long time to Anahuac. They grew to supremacy in part probably by the arrival of new immigrants, but chiefly by conquest of the small states into which the country was divided. They could learn from their more cultivated neighbors to reform their calendar, compute time with greater accuracy, and make important improvements in other respects. They must also have modified their religious system to some extent, for it does not appear that they had adopted the worship of Kukulcan (whose name they transformed into Quetzalcohuatl) before they came to Mexico. But they brought with them an effective political organization, and very likely they were better fitted than most of their new neighbors for the rude work of war.

Before the city of Mexico was built, the seat of their government was at Tezcuco. The character of their civilization after they rose to pre-eminence was shown in their organization, in their skill as builders, in the varied forms of their industry, and in the development of their religious ceremonies. It is manifest that they adopted all the astronomical knowledge and appliances found in the neighboring states which they subjugated. Their measure of the solar year and their numbering of the months were precisely like what had long existed in this part of the country; and they had the same astronomical implements or contrivances. One of these contrivances, found at Chapultepec, is described as follows:

"On the horizontal plane of a large, carefully-worked stone, three arrows were cut in relief, so that the shaft ends came together and made equal angles in the centre. The points were directed eastward, the two outside showing the two solstitial points, and that in the centre the equinoctial. A line on the carved band holding them together was in range with holes in two stones which stood exactly north and south. A cord drawn tightly through the holes in these two stones would, at the moment of noon, cast its shadow on the line drawn across the band. It was a perfect instrument for ascertaining east and west with precision, and for determining the exact time by the rising and setting of the sun at the equinoxes and solstices. This stone has now been broken up and used to construct a furnace."

These Aztecs were manifestly something very different from "Mexican savages." At the same time, they were less advanced in many things than their predecessors. Their skill in architecture and architectural ornamentation did not enable them to build such cities as Mitla and Palenque, and their "picture writing" was a much ruder form of the graphic art than the phonetic system of the Mayas and Quichés. It does not appear that they ever went so far in literary improvement as to adopt this simpler and more complete system for any purpose whatever. If the country had never, in the previous ages, felt the influence of a higher culture than that of the Aztecs, it would not have now, and never could have had, ruined cities like Mitla, Copan, and Palenque. Not only was the system of writing shown by the countless inscriptions quite beyond the attainments of Aztec art, but also the abundant sculptures and the whole system of decoration found in the old ruins.

X.

ANCIENT PERU.

The ruins of Ancient Peru are found chiefly on the elevated table-lands of the Andes, between Quito and Lake Titicaca; but they can be traced five hundred miles farther south, to Chili, and throughout the region connecting these high plateaus with the Pacific coast. The great district to which they belong extends north and south about two thousand miles. When the marauding Spaniards arrived in the country, this whole region was the seat of a populous and prosperous empire, complete in its civil organization, supported by an efficient system of industry, and presenting a very notable development of some of the more important arts of civilized life. These ruins differ from those in Mexico and Central America. No inscriptions are found in Peru; there is no longer a "marvelous abundance of decorations;" nothing is seen like the monoliths of Copan or the bas-reliefs of Palenque. The method of building is different; the Peruvian temples were not high truncated pyramids, and the great edifices were not erected on pyramidal foundations. The Peruvian ruins show us remains of cities, temples, palaces, other edifices of various kinds, fortresses, aqueducts (one of them four hundred and fifty miles long), great roads (extending through the whole length of the empire), and terraces on the sides of mountains. For all these constructions the builders used cut stone laid in mortar or cement, and their work was done admirably, but it is every where seen that the masonry, although sometimes ornamented, was generally plain in style and always massive. The antiquities in this region have not been as much explored and described as those north of the isthmus, but their general character is known, and particular descriptions of some of them have been published.

THE SPANISH HUNT FOR PERU.

The Spanish conquest of Peru furnishes one of the most remarkable chapters in the history of audacious villainy. It was the work of successful buccaneers as unscrupulous as any crew of pirates that ever robbed and murdered on the ocean. After their settlements began on the islands and the Atlantic coast, rumors came to them of a wonderful country somewhere at a distance in the west. They knew nothing of another ocean between them and the Indies; the western side of the continent was a veiled land of mystery, but the rumors, constantly repeated, assured them that there was a country in that unknown region where gold was more abundant than iron among themselves. Their strongest passions were moved; greed for the precious metals and thirst for adventures.

Balboa was hunting for Peru when he discovered the Pacific, about 1511 A.D. He was guided across the isthmus by a young native chief, who told him of that ocean, saying it was the best way to the country where all the common household utensils were made of gold. At the Bay of Panama Balboa heard more of Peru, and went down the coast to find it, but did not go south much beyond the eighth degree of north latitude. In his company of adventurers at this time was Francisco Pizarro, by whom Peru was found, subjugated, robbed, and ruined, some fifteen or twenty years later. Balboa was superseded by Pedrarias, another greedy adventurer, whose jealousy arrested his operations and finally put him to death. The town of Panama was founded in 1519 by this Pedrarias, chiefly as a point on the Pacific from which he could seek and attack Peru. Under his direction, in 1522, the search was attempted by Pascual de Andagoya, but he failed to get down the coast beyond the limit of Balboa's exploration. Meanwhile clearer and more abundant reports of the rich and marvelous nation to be found somewhere below that point were circulated among the Spaniards, and their eagerness to reach it became intense.

In 1524, three men could have been seen in Panama busily engaged preparing another expedition to go in search of the golden country. These were Francisco Pizarro, a bold and capable adventurer, who could neither read nor write; Diego de Almagro, an impulsive, passionate, reckless soldier of fortune, and Hernando de Luque, a Spanish ecclesiastic, Vicar of Panama, and a man well acquainted with the world and skilled in reading character, acting at this time, it is said, for another person who kept out of view. They had formed an alliance to discover and rob Peru. Luque would furnish most of the funds, and wait in Panama for the others to do the work. Pizarro would be commander-in-chief. The vessels used would necessarily be such as could be built at Panama, and, therefore, not very efficient.

Pizarro went down the coast, landing from time to time to explore and rob villages, until he reached about the fourth degree of north latitude, when he was obliged to return for supplies and repairs. It became necessary to reconstruct the contract and allow Pedrarias an interest in it. On the next voyage, one of the vessels went half a degree south of the equator, and encountered a vessel " like a European caravel," which was, in fact, a Peruvian *balsa*, loaded with merchandise, vases, mirrors of burnished silver, and curious fabrics of cotton and woolen.

It became again indispensable to send back to Panama for supplies and repairs, and Pizarro was doomed to wait for them seven months on an island. He next visited Tumbez, in Peru, and went to the ninth degree of south latitude; but he was obliged to visit Spain to get necessary aid before he could attempt any thing more, and it was not until the year 1531 that the conquest of Peru was actually undertaken.

In 1531 Pizarro finally entered Tumbez with his buccaneers, and marched into the country, sending word to the Inca that he came to aid him against his enemies. There had been a civil war in the country, which had been divided by the great Inca, Huayna Capac, the conqueror of Quito, between his two sons, Huascar and Atahuallpa, and Huascar had been defeated and thrown into prison, and finally put to death. At a city called Caxamalca, Pizarro contrived, by means of the most atrocious treachery, to seize the Inca and massacre some ten thousand of the principal Peruvians, who came to his camp unarmed on a friendly visit. This threw the whole empire into confusion, and made the conquest easy. The Inca filled a room with gold as the price of his ransom; the Spaniards took the gold, broke their promise, and put him to death.

THE RUINS NEAR LAKE TITICACA.

It is now agreed that the Peruvian antiquities represent two distinct periods in the ancient history of the country, one being much older than the other. Mr. Prescott accepts and repeats the opinion that "there existed in the country a race advanced in civilization before the time of the Incas," and that the ruins on the shores of Lake Titicaca are older than the reign of the first Inca. In the work of Rivero and Von Tschudi, it is stated that a critical examination of the monuments "indicates two very different epochs in Peruvian art, at least so far as concerns architecture; one before and the other after the arrival of the first Inca." Among the ruins which belong to the older civilization are those at Lake Titicaca, old Huannco, Tiahuanaco, and Gran-Chimu, and it probably originated the roads and aqueducts. At Cuzco and other places are remains of buildings which represent the later time; but Cuzco of the Incas appears to have occupied the site of a ruined city

Peruvian Ruins. 227

of the older period. Figure 51 gives a view of the ancient Peruvian masonry. Montesinos supposes the name of Cuzco was derived from *cosca*, a Peruvian word signifying to level, or from heaps of earth called *coscos*, which abounded there. In his account of the previous times there is mention that an old city built there was in ruins. Perhaps the first Inca found on its site nothing but *coscos*, or heaps of ruins.

Fig. 51.—Ancient Peruvian Masonry.

At Lake Titicaca some of the more important remains are on the islands. On Titicaca Island are the ruins of a great edifice described as "a palace or temple." Remains of other structures exist, but their ruins are old, much older than the time of the Incas. Figures 52 and 53 represent different ruins on the island of

Fig. 52.—Ruins of "Temple" on the Island of Titicaca.

Titicaca. They were all built of hewn stone, and had doors and windows, with posts, sills, and thresholds of

Fig. 63.—Ruins on Tiburon Island.

stone, the doorways being narrower above than below. On the island of Coati there are remarkable ruins. The largest building here is also described as "a palace or temple," although it may have been something else. It was not high, but very large in extent. It stood around three sides of a parallelogram, with some peculiarities of construction connected with the ends or wings. Making allowance for the absence of the pyramidal foundations, it has more resemblance to some of the great constructions in Central America than to any thing peculiar to the later period of Peruvian architecture. Another ruin on this island is shown in Figure 54. The antiqui-

Fig. 54.—Ruins on the Island of Coati.

ties on the islands and shores of this lake need to be more completely explored and described, and probably interesting discoveries could be made at some points by means of well-directed excavations.

A few miles from Lake Titicaca, at Tiahuanaco, are ruins which were very imposing when first seen by the Spaniards in the time of Pizarro. It is usual to speak of them as the oldest ruins in Peru, which may or may not be correct. They must, however, be classed with those at the lake. Not much now remains of the edifices, which were in a very ruinous condition three hundred and forty years ago. They were described by Cieça de Leon, who accompanied Pizarro, and also by Diego d'Alcobaça. Cieça de Leon mentions "great edifices" that were in ruins, "an artificial hill raised on a groundwork of stone," and "two stone idols resembling the human figure, and apparently made by skillful artificers." These "idols" were great statues, ten or twelve feet high. One of them, which was carried to La Paz in 1842, measured "three and a half yards" in length. Sculptured decorations appear on them, and, according to Cieça de Leon, the figures seemed to be "clothed in long vestments" different from those worn in the time of the Incas. Of a very remarkable edifice, whose foundations could be traced near these statues, nothing remained then "but a well-built wall, which must have been there for ages, the stones being very much worn and crumbled." Cieça de Leon's description goes on as follows:

"In this place, also, there are stones so large and so overgrown that our wonder is incited, it being incomprehensible how the power of man could have placed them where we see them. They are variously wrought, and some of them, having the form of men, must have been idols. Near the walls are many caves and excavations under the earth, but in another place, farther west, are other and greater monuments, such as large gateways with hinges, platforms, and porches, each made of a sin-

Peruvian Ruins. 233

gle stone. It surprised me to see these enormous gateways made of great masses of stone, some of which were thirty feet long, fifteen high, and six thick."

Many of the stone monuments at Tiahuanaco have been removed, some for building, some for other purposes. In one case, "large masses of sculptured stone ten yards in length and six in width" were used to make grinding stones for a chocolate mill. The principal monuments now seen on this field of ruins are a vast mound covering several acres, where there seems to have been a great edifice, fragments of columns, erect slabs of stone which formed parts of buildings, and several of the monolithic gateways, the largest of which was made of a single stone ten feet high and thirteen broad. Figure 55 gives a view of one. The doorway is six feet four inches

Fig. 55.—Monolithic Gateway at Tiahuanaco.

high, and three feet two inches wide. Above it, along the whole length of the stone, which is now broken, is a cornice covered with sculptured figures. "The whole neighborhood," says Mr. Squier, "is strewn with immense blocks of stone elaborately wrought, equaling, if not surpassing in size, any known to exist in Egypt or India."

At Cuzco, two or more degrees north of Lake Titicaca, there are ruins of buildings that were occupied until the rule of the Incas was overthrown. Remains of the old structures are seen in various parts of the present town, some of them incorporated into new edifices built by the Spaniards. Cyclopean remains of walls of the Temple of the Sun now constitute a portion of the Convent of St. Domingo. In the days of the Incas, this temple stood "a circuit of more than four hundred paces," and was surrounded by a great wall built of cut stone. Remains of

Fig. 56.—Remains of Fortress Walls at Cuzco.

the old fortifications are seen; and there is an extensive ruin here which shows what is supposed to be all that remains of the palace of the Incas. Figures 56 and 57 give views of remains of the ancient fortress walls at

Fig. 56.—End View of Fortress Walls at Cuzco.

Cuzco. Occasionally there is search at Cuzco, by means of excavation, for antiquities. Within a few years an important discovery has been made; a lunar calendar of the Incas, made of gold, has been exhumed. At first it was described as "a gold breastplate or sun;" but William Bollaert, who gives an account of it, finds that it is a calendar, the first discovered in Peru. Many others, probably, went to the melting-pot at the time of the Conquest. This is not quite circular. The outer ring is five inches and three tenths in diameter, and the inner four inches. It was made to be fastened to the breast of an Inca or priest. The figures were stamped on it, and there "seem to be twenty-four compartments, large and small, including three at the top. At the bottom are two spaces; figures may or may not have been there, but it looks as if they had been worn away." It was found about the year 1859.

The uniform and constant report of Peruvian tradition places the beginning of this old civilization in the Valley of Cuzco, near Lake Titicaca. There appeared the first civilizers and the first civilized communities. This beautiful valley is the most elevated table-land on the continent, Lake Titicaca being 12,846 feet above the sea level. Were it not within the tropics, it would be a region of eternal snow, for it is more than 4000 feet higher than the beginning of perpetual snow on Mont Blanc. Near it are some of the higher peaks of the Andes, among them Sorato, Illimani, and Sabama.

OTHER RUINS IN PERU.

The ancient Peru conquered and robbed by Pizarro is now divided into Ecuador, Peru, Bolivia, and Chili as far down as the thirty-seventh degree of south latitude. Its remains are found to some extent in all these countries, although most abundantly in Peru.

The ruins known as "the Palaces of Gran-Chimu" are situated in the northwestern part of Peru, near Truxillo. Here, in the time of the first Incas, was an independent state, which was subjugated by the Inca set down in the list of Montesinos as the grandfather of Huayna Capac, about a century before the Spaniards arrived. For what is known of these ruins we are chiefly indebted to Mariano Rivero, director of the National Museum at Lima. They cover a space of three quarters of a league, without including the walled squares found on every side. The chief objects of interest are the remains of two great edifices called palaces. "These palaces are immense areas surrounded by high walls of brick, the walls being now ten or twelve yards high and six feet thick at the base." There was in each case another wall exterior to this. Within the palace walls were squares and dwellings, with narrow passages between them, and the walls are decorated. In the largest palace are the remains of a great reservoir for water, which was brought to it by subterranean aqueducts from the River Moche, two miles distant. Outside the inclosures of these palaces are remains of a vast number of buildings, which indicate that the city contained a great population. The Spaniards took vast quantities of gold from the *huacas* or tombs at this place. The amount taken from a single tomb in the years 1566 and 1592 was officially estimated at nearly a million dollars. Figure 58 presents an end view of

Fig. 58.—End View of Walls at Gran-Chimu.

the walls at Gran-Chimu. Figures 59 and 60 represent some of the decorations at Chimu-Canchu.

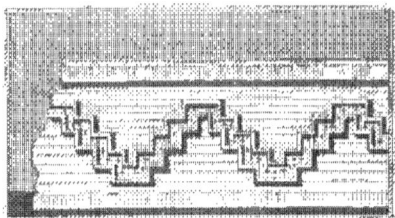

Figs. 59 and 60.—Decorations at Chimu-Canchu.

Remarkable ruins exist at Cuelap, in Northern Peru. "They consist of a wall of wrought stones 3600 feet long, 560 broad, and 150 high, constituting a solid mass with a level summit." Probably the interior was made of earth. On this mass was another, "600 feet long, 500 broad, and 150 high." In this, and also in the lower structure, there are many rooms made of wrought stone, in which are a great number of niches or cells one or two yards deep, which were used as tombs. Other old structures exist in that neighborhood. Farther south, at Huanuco el Viego, or Old Huanuco, are two peculiar edifices and a terrace, and near them the faded traces of a large town. The two edifices were built of a composition of pebbles and clay, faced with hewn stone. One of them is called the "Look-out," but it is impossible to discover the purpose for which it was built. The interior of the other is crossed by six walls, in each of which is

Fig. 81.—Edifice, with Gateway, at Old Huanuco.

a gateway, the outer one being finely finished, and showing a sculptured animal on each of the upper corners. It has a large court, and rooms made of cut stones. Connected with this structure was a well-built aqueduct.

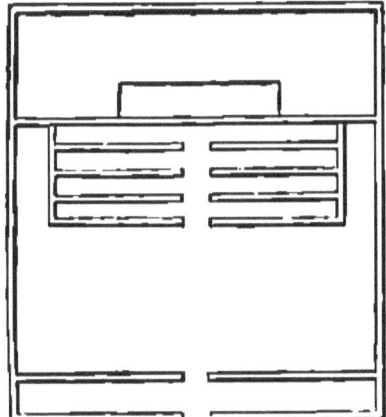

Fig. 62.—Ground Plan of Edifice at Old Huanuco.

Figures 61 and 62 give views of the so-called palace and its ground plan. Figure 63 represents the Look-out.

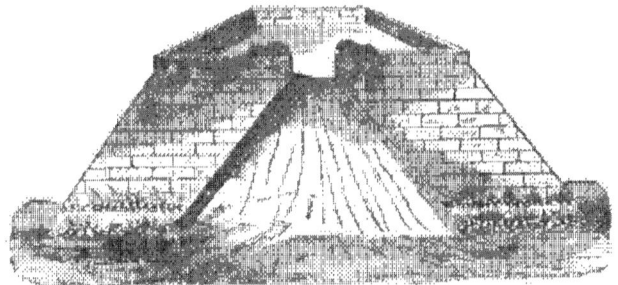

Fig. 63.—"Look-out" at Old Huanuco.

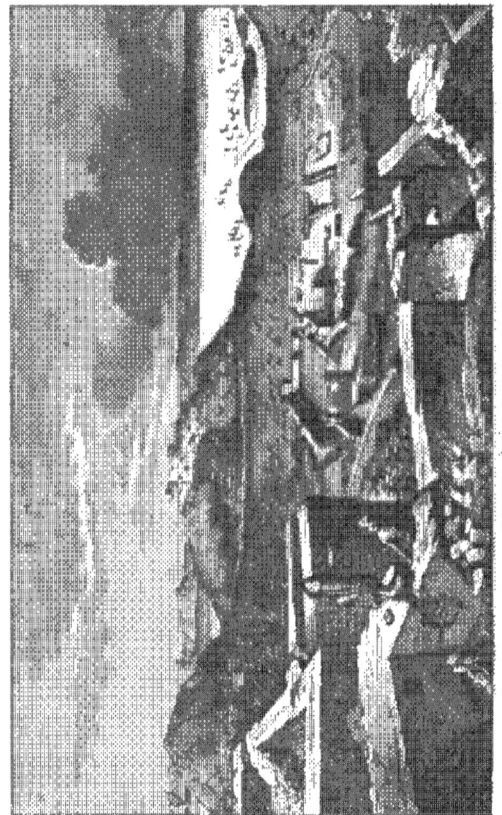

Fig. 64.—Shrine at Pachacama.

Seven leagues from Lima, near the sea, are the much-dilapidated ruins, shown in Figure 64, of a large city of the Incas, which was built chiefly of adobes or sun-dried bricks. It is called Pachacamac. Ruins of towns, castles, fortresses, and other structures are found all about the country. At one place, near Chavin de Huanta, there are remarkable ruins which are very old. The material used here was like that seen at Old Huanuco. From the interior of one of the great buildings there is a subterranean passage which, it is said, goes under the river to the opposite bank. Very ancient ruins, showing remains of large and remarkable edifices, were seen near Huamanga, and described by Cicça de Leon. The native traditions said this city was built by "bearded white men, who came there long before the time of the Incas, and established a settlement." It is noticed every where that the ancient Peruvians made large use of aqueducts, which they built with notable skill, using hewn stones and cement, and making them very substantial. Some of them are still in use. They were used to carry water to the cities and to irrigate the cultivated lands. A few of them were very long. There is mention of one which was a hundred and fifty miles long, and of another which was extended four hundred and fifty miles across sierras and over rivers, from south to north.

THE GREAT PERUVIAN ROADS.

Nothing in Ancient Peru was more remarkable than the public roads. No ancient people has left traces of works more astonishing than these, so vast was their extent, and so great the skill and labor required to construct them. One of these roads ran along the mountains through the whole length of the empire, from Quito to Chili. Another, starting from this at Cuzco, went down to the coast and extended northward to the equator. These roads were built on beds or "deep under-structures" of masonry. The width of the roadways varied from twenty to twenty-five feet, and they were made level and smooth by paving, and in some places by a sort of macadamizing with pulverized stone mixed with lime and bituminous cement. This cement was used in all the masonry. On each side of the roadway was "a very strong wall more than a fathom in thickness." These roads went over marshes, rivers, and great chasms of the sierras, and through rocky precipices and mountain sides. The great road passing along the mountains was a marvelous work. In many places its way was cut through rock for leagues. Great ravines were filled up with solid masonry. Rivers were crossed by means of a curious kind of suspension bridges, and no obstruction was encountered which the builders did not overcome. The builders of our Pacific Railroad, with their superior engineering skill and mechanical appliances, might reasonably shrink from the cost and the difficulties of such a work as this. Extending from one degree north of Quito to Cuzco, and from Cuzco to Chili, it was quite as long as the two Pacific railroads, and its wild route among the mountains was far more difficult.

Sarmiento, describing it, said, "It seems to me that if the emperor (Charles V.) should see fit to order the construction of another road like that which leads from Quito to Cuzco, or that which from Cuzco goes toward Chili, I certainly think he would not be able to make it, with all his power." Humboldt examined some of the remains of this road, and described as follows a portion of it seen in a pass of the Andes, between Mansi and Loxa: "Our eyes rested continually on superb remains of a paved road of the Incas. The roadway, paved with well-cut, dark porphyritic stone, was twenty feet wide, and rested on deep foundations. This road was marvelous. None of the Roman roads I have seen in Italy, in the South of France, or in Spain, appeared to me more imposing than this work of the ancient Peruvians." He saw remains of several other shorter roads which were built in the same way, some of them between Loxa and the River Amazon. Along these roads at equal distances were edifices, a kind of caravanseras, built of hewn stone, for the accommodation of travelers.

These great works were described by every Spanish writer on Peru, and in some accounts of them we find suggestions in regard to their history. They are called "roads of the Incas," but they were probably much older than the time of these rulers. The mountain road running toward Quito was much older than the Inca Huayna Capac, to whom it has sometimes been attributed. It is stated that when he started by this route to invade the Quitús, the road was so bad that "he found great difficulties in the passage." It was then an old road, much out of repair, and he immediately ordered the necessary reconstructions. Gomara says, "Huayna

Capac restored, enlarged, and completed these roads, but he did not build them, as some pretend." These great artificial highways were broken up and made useless at the time of the Conquest, and the subsequent barbarous rule of the Spaniards allowed them to go to decay. Now only broken remains of them exist to show their former character.

THE PERUVIAN CIVILIZATION.

The development of civilization in Peru was very different from that in Mexico and Central America. In both regions the people were sun-worshipers, but their religious organizations, as well as their methods of building temples, were unlike. Neither of these peoples seems to have borrowed from the other. It may be that all the old American civilizations had a common origin in South America, and that all the ancient Americans whose civilization can be traced in remains found north of the Isthmus came originally from that part of the continent. This hypothesis appears to me more probable than any other I have heard suggested. But, assuming this to be true, the first migration of civilized people from South America must have taken place at a very distant period in the past, for it preceded not only the history indicated by the existing antiquities, but also an earlier history, during which the Peruvians and Central Americans grew to be as different from their ancestors as from each other. In each case, the development of civilization represented by existing monuments, so far as we can study it, appears to have been original.

In some respects the Peruvian civilization was developed to such a degree as challenged admiration. The Peruvians were highly skilled in agriculture and in some kinds of manufactures. No people ever had a more efficient system of industry. This created their wealth and made possible their great public works. All accounts of the country at the time of the Conquest agree in the statement that they cultivated the soil in a very admirable way and with remarkable success, using aqueducts for irrigation, and employing guano as one of their most important fertilizers. Europeans learned from them the value of this fertilizer, and its name, *guano*, is Peruvian. The remains of their works show what they were as builders. Their skill in cutting stone and their wonderful masonry can be seen and admired by modern builders in what is left of their aqueducts, their roads, their temples, and their other great edifices.

They had great proficiency in the arts of spinning, weaving, and dyeing. For their cloth they used cotton and the wool of four varieties of the llama, that of the vicuña being the finest. Some of their cloth had interwoven designs and ornaments very skillfully executed. Many of their fabrics had rare excellence in the eyes of the Spaniards. Garcilasso says, "The coverings of the beds were blankets and friezes of the wool of the vicuña, which is so fine and so much prized that, among other precious things from that land, they have been brought for the bed of Don Philip II." Of their dyes, this account is given in the work of Rivero and Von Tschudi:

"They possessed the secret of fixing the dye of all

colors, flesh-color, yellow, gray, blue, green, black, etc., so firmly in the thread, or in the cloth already woven, that they never faded during the lapse of ages, even when exposed to the air or buried (in tombs) under ground. Only the cotton became slightly discolored, while the woolen fabrics preserved their primitive lustre. It is a circumstance worth remarking that chemical analyses made of pieces of cloth of all the different dyes prove that the Peruvians extracted all their colors from the vegetable and none from the mineral kingdom. In fact, the natives of the Peruvian mountains now use plants unknown to Europeans, producing from them bright and lasting colors."

They had great skill in the art of working metals, especially gold and silver. Besides these precious metals, they had copper, tin, lead, and quicksilver. Figures 65 and 66 show some of the implements used by the Peruvians. Iron was unknown to them in the time of the Incas, although some maintain that they had it in the previous ages, to which belong the ruins at Lake Titicaca. Iron ore was and still is very abundant in Peru. It is impossible to conceive how the Peruvians were able to cut and work stone in such a masterly way, or to construct their great roads and aqueducts without the use of iron tools. Some of the languages of the country, and perhaps all, had names for iron; in official Peruvian it was called *quillay*, and in the old Chilian tongue *panilic*. "It is remarkable," observes Molina, "that iron, which has been thought unknown to the ancient Americans, has particular names in some of their tongues." It is not easy to understand why they had names for this metal, if they never at any

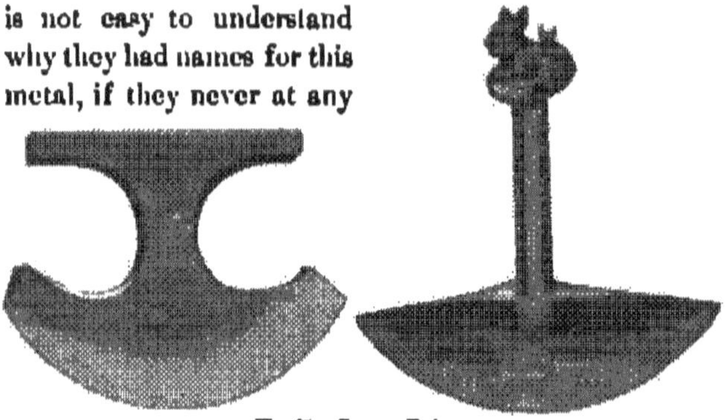

Fig. 65.—Copper Knives.

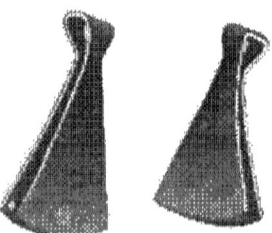
Fig. 66.—Copper Tweezers.

time had knowledge of the metal itself. In the Mercurio Peruano, tome i., p. 201, 1791, it is stated that, anciently, the Peruvian sovereigns "worked magnificent iron mines at Ancoriames, on the west shore of Lake Titicaca;" but I can not give the evidence used in support of this statement.

Their goldsmiths and silversmiths had attained very great proficiency. They could melt the metals in furnaces, cast them in moulds made of clay and gypsum, hammer their work with remarkable dexterity, inlay it, and solder it with great perfection. The gold and silver work of these artists was extremely abundant in the country at the time of the Conquest, but Spanish greed had it all melted for coinage. It was with articles of this gold-work that the Inca Atahuallpa filled a room in his vain endeavor to purchase release from captivity. One of the old chroniclers mentions "statuary, jars, vases, and every species of vessels, all of fine gold." Describing one of the palaces, he said: "They had an artificial garden, the soil of which was made of small pieces of fine gold, and this was artificially sowed with different kinds of maize which were of gold, their stems, leaves, and ears. Besides this, they had more than twenty sheep (llamas), with their lambs, attended by shepherds, all made of gold." This may be the same artificial garden which was mentioned by Francisco Lopez de Gomara, who places it on "an island near Puna." Similar gardens of gold are mentioned by others. It is believed that a large quantity of Peruvian gold-work was thrown into Lake Titicaca to keep it from the Spanish robbers. In a description of one lot of golden articles sent to Spain in 1534 by Pizarro, there is mention of "four llamas, ten statues of women of full size, and a cistern of gold so curious that it incited the wonder of all."

Nothing is more constantly mentioned by the old Spanish chroniclers than the vast abundance of gold in Peru. It was more common than any other metal. Temples and palaces were covered with it, and it was very beautifully wrought into ornaments, temple furniture, articles for household use, and imitations of almost every object in nature. In the course of twenty-five years after the Conquest, the Spaniards sent from Peru to Spain more than four hundred million ducats (900,000,000 dollars) worth of gold, all or nearly all of it having been taken from the subjugated Peruvians as "booty."

Figures 67 and 68 show a golden and a silver vase, reduced from the actual

Fig. 67.—Golden Vase.

Fig. 68.—Silver Vase.

size. Figures 69 and 70 represent various articles of pottery; all these illustrations are copies from articles taken from old Peruvian tombs.

The most perfectly manufactured articles of Peruvian pottery were used in the tombs. Some of those made for other uses were very curious. A considerable number of articles made for common use have been preserved. Mariano Rivero, a Peruvian, says: "At this day there exist in many houses pitchers, large jars, and earthen pots of this manufacture, which are preferred for their solidity to those manufactured by our own potters." The ancient Peruvians were inferior to the Central Americans in the arts of ornamentation and sculpture.

Science among the Peruvians was not very highly de-

Fig. 6.—Articles of Pottery.

veloped, but engineering skill of some kind is indicated by the great roads and aqueducts. Their knowledge of the art of preparing colors and certain useful medicines implied a study of plants. Their progress in astronomy was not equal to that found in Central America; nevertheless, they had an accurate measure of the solar year, but, unlike the Central Americans, they divided the year into twelve months, and they used mechanical contrivances successfully to fix the times of the solstices and equinoxes. A class of men called *amautas* was trained to preserve and teach whatever knowledge existed in the country. It was their business to understand the *quippus*, keep in memory the historical poems, give attention to the science and practice of medicine, and train their pupils in knowledge.

Fig. 76.—Articles of Pottery.

These were not priests; they were the "learned men" of Peru, and the government allowed them every facility for study and for communicating instruction. How much they knew of astronomy it is not easy to say. They had knowledge of some of the planets, and it is claimed that there is some reason to believe they used aids to eyesight in studying the heavens, such as some suppose were used by our Mound-Builders. A discovery made in Bolivia a few years since is cited in support of this belief. It is the figure of a man in the act of using a tube to aid vision, which was taken from an ancient tomb. Mr. David Forbes, an English chemist and geologist, obtained it in Bolivia, and carried it to England in 1864. William Bollaert describes it as follows in a paper read to the London Anthropological Society:

"It is a nude figure, of silver, two inches and a half in height, on a flat, pointed pedestal. In the right hand it has the mask of a human face, but in the left a tube over half an inch in length, the narrow part placed to the left eye in a diagonal position, as if observing some celestial object. This is the first specimen of a figure in the act of looking through a hollow tube directed to the heavens that has been found in the New World. We can not suppose the Peruvians had any thing that more nearly resembled a telescope. It was found in a chulpa, or ancient Indian tomb, at Caquingora, near Corocoro (lat. 17° 15′ S., and long. 68° 35′ W.), in Bolivia." He forgets the astronomical monument described by Captain Dupaix.

The art of writing in alphabetical characters, so far as appears, was unknown to the Peruvians in the time of the Incas. No Peruvian books existed at that time, and no inscriptions have been found in any of the ruins. They had a method of recording events, keeping accounts, and making reports to the government by means of the *quippu*. This was made of cords of twisted wool fastened to a base prepared for the purpose. These cords were of various sizes and colors, and every size and color had its meaning. The record was made by means of an elaborate system of knots and artificial intertwinings. The *amautas* were carefully educated to the business of understanding and using the *quippus*, and "this science was so much perfected that those skilled in it attained the art of recording historical events, laws, and decrees, so as to transmit to their descendants the most striking events of the empire; thus the *quippus* could supply the place of documents." Each *quippu* was a book full of information for those who could read it.

Among the *amautas* memory was educated to retain and transmit to posterity songs, historical narratives, and long historical poems. It is said, also, that tragedies and comedies were composed and preserved in this way, and that dramatic performances were among the regular entertainments encouraged and supported by the Incas. Whether the art of writing ever existed in the country can not now be determined. Some of the Peruvian tongues had names for paper; the people knew that a kind of paper or parchment could be made of plantain leaves, and, according to Montesinos, writing and books were common in the older times, that is to say, in ages long previous to the Incas. He explains how the art was lost, as I shall presently show.

It is not improbable that a kind of hieroglyphical writing existed in some of the Peruvian communities, especially among the Aymaracs. Humboldt mentions books of hieroglyphical writing found among the Panocs, on the River Ucayali, which were "bundles of their paper resembling our volumes in quarto." A Franciscan missionary found an old man sitting at the foot of a palm-tree and reading one of these books to several young persons. The Franciscan was told that the writing "contained hidden things which no stranger ought to know." It was seen that the pages of the book were "covered with figures of men, animals, and isolated characters, deemed hieroglyphical, and arranged in lines with order and symmetry." The Panocs said these books "were transmitted to them by their ancestors, and had relation to wanderings and ancient wars." There is similar writing on a prepared llama skin found among other antiquities on a peninsula in Lake Titicaca, which is now in the museum at La Paz, Bolivia. It appears to be a record of atrocities perpetrated by the Spaniards at the time of the Conquest, and shows that some of the Aymaracs could at that time write hieroglyphica.

XI.

PERUVIAN ANCIENT HISTORY.

The Peruvians, like most other important peoples in all ages, had mythical wonder-stories instead of authentic ancient history to explain the origin of their nation. These were told in traditions and legends preserved and transmitted from generation to generation by the *amautas*. If they were also recorded in secret books of hieroglyphical writing, such as those found among the Panoes on the Ucayali, which "contained hidden things that no stranger ought to know," satisfactory evidence of the fact has never been brought to light. In addition to these, they had many historical traditions of much more importance, related in long poems and preserved in the same way; and there were annals and national documents recorded in the *quippus*.

Some of the Spanish writers on Peru, who described what they saw in the country at the time of the Conquest, discussed its history. If they had used the proper sources of information with a more penetrating and complete investigation, and studied the subject as it might have been studied at that time, their historical sketches would now have great value. The two most important works written at this time, the "Relacion" of Sarmiento and the "Relaciones" of Polo de Ondegardo, were never printed. But none of these writers sought to study Peruvian antiquity beyond the period of the Incas, although some of them (Acosta for instance) inquired sufficiently to see that Manco Capac was a mythical personage prefixed to the dynastic line of the Incas without actually belonging to it. This limited view of the ancient history, which was inconsistent with what could be seen in the antiquities and traditions of the country, was generally accepted, because nothing more could be known in Europe, and its influence was established by the undue importance accorded to the "Commentarios Reales" of Garcilasso de la Vega, published in 1609.

GARCILASSO'S HISTORY.

Garcilasso de la Vega, the son of a distinguished Spaniard of the same name, was born at Cuzco in 1540. His mother, named Ñusta, was a niece of the great Inca Huayna Capac, and granddaughter of his no less eminent predecessor, Tupac Yupanqui. The intimate blood relationship which connected him with the Incas naturally drew attention to his work, and, with more haste than reason, was treated as the best possible qualification for writing Peruvian history; therefore his "Commentarios" acquired a very great celebrity, and came to be regarded as the highest authority on all questions relating to Peru previous to the Conquest. The work never deserved this reputation, although it was not without value as an addition to what had been written on the subject by Spaniards. Garcilasso was not well qualified to write a faithful history of Peru either by his knowledge or by the temper of his mind. His aim was to glorify the Incas and their times, and much of his work was in the strain of tales heard in childhood from his mother.

The "Commentarios Reales" were written just as their author's training had prepared him to write them. He lived in Cuzco without education until he was nearly twenty years old, his intellectual development being confined to the instruction necessary to make him a good Catholic. He then went to Spain and never returned to Peru. The next period of his life was devoted to seeking distinction in the Spanish military service; but political influence was against him, and he could not attain the object of his ambition. He finally retired to Cordova, acquired some literary culture, and resolved to win distinction by writing a history of his native country. His materials for such a history, in addition to what could be learned from the earlier Spanish writers, consisted entirely of what he had learned of his mother and his early Peruvian associates at Cuzco, and of such acquisitions as could be gained by means of correspondence with his acquaintances in Peru, after the purpose to write a history was formed. It can be seen readily that Garcilasso's history written in this way might have a certain value, while it could not be safely accepted as an authority. The first part of his work was published in 1609, when he was nearly seventy years old.

According to his version of the Peruvian annals, the rule of the Incas began with the mythical Manco Capac, and lasted over five hundred years; and this version, with some variations in estimates of the time, has been repeated ever since. The dynastic line of the Incas thus determined is given in the work of Rivero and Von Tschudi as follows:

1. Manco-Capac, mysterious "son of the sun," who began to reign in 1021 A.D., and died in 1062, having reigned forty years. 2. Sinchi-Rocca, who reigned thirty years, from 1062 to 1091. 3. Lloque-Yupanqui, reigned thirty-five years, from 1091 to 1126. 4. Mayta-Capac, thirty years, from 1126 to 1156. 5. Capac-Yupanqui, forty-one years, from 1156 to 1197. 6. Inca Rocca, fifty-one years, from 1197 to 1249. 7. Yahuar-Capac, forty years, from 1249 to 1289. 8. Viracocha, fifty-one years, from 1289 to 1340; his son Inca Urco reigned after him eleven days, and was then deposed "as a fool incapable of governing." 9. Titu-Manco-Capac-Pachacutec, sixty years, from 1340 to 1400, living, says tradition, to be one hundred and three years old. 10. Yupanqui, thirty-nine years, from 1400 to 1439. 11. Tupac-Yupanqui (Garcilasso's great-grandfather) thirty-six years, from 1439 to 1475. 12. Huayna-Capac, "the most glorious of the Incas," fifty years, from 1475 to 1525. After his death the empire was divided between his two sons Huascar and Atahuallpa. This caused a civil war, which ended with the death of Huascar in 1532. One year later Atahuallpa was himself destroyed by Cortez.

Manco-Capac, here set down as the first Inca, with a marvelous story of his mysterious origin and his miraculous powers as a civilizer, was undoubtedly borrowed from traditions of the origin of civilization in the more ancient times, which had been used by the Incas in support of their claim to direct descent from the sun. In reality, the first Inca was Rocca, or Sinchi-Rocca, and several of the early Spanish writers were sufficiently well informed to see this. The period of the Incas must have been less than five hundred years if their dynasty consisted of no more than twelve or thirteen sovereigns. In other respects, this table of the sovereigns may be substantially correct, for there is a general agreement in regard to the names and the order of succession, although Montesinos maintains that the fifth Inca on the list was borrowed by Garcilasso from traditions of a much more ancient sovereign who was greatly celebrated in the historical poems, or confounded with him. The period of the Incas was very distinct in Peruvian history, but it is now understood that they represent only the last period in the history of a civilization which began much farther back in the past.

FERNANDO MONTESINOS.

The only Spanish writer who really studied the ancient history of Peru in the traditional and other records of the country was Fernando Montesinos, who went there about a century after the Conquest. He was sent from Spain on service which took him to every part of Peru, and gave him the best possible opportunities for investigation. He was a scholar and a worker, with a strong inclination to such studies, and, during two periods of residence in the country, he devoted fifteen years to these inquiries with unremitting industry and great success. He soon learned to communicate freely with the Peruvians in their own language; then he applied himself to collect the historical poems, narratives, and traditions. He succeeded in getting assistance from many of the older men who had learned of the *amautas*, and especially of those who were trained to read the *quippus*. Nothing was omitted which could aid his purpose. In this way Montesinos made a great collection of what may be called the *old Peruvian documents*, and gained a vast amount of information which no other writer had used or even sought to acquire.

The materials collected were more important than is at once understood by those accustomed to depend wholly on writing and printing for the preservation of literature, because they can not easily realize to what extent the faculty of memory may be sharpened and developed by a class of men devoted to this culture in communities where such mechanical aids do not exist. It is known that long poems, stories, and historical narratives have been preserved by unlettered peoples much below the civilized condition of the Peruvians. Long poems, extending to three and four hundred lines, were retained by memory, and transmitted from generation to generation among the Sandwich Islanders. Many scholars have believed that all the early literature of Greece, including the Iliad, the Odyssey, and all other "poems of the Cycle," was preserved in this way by the Rhapsodists for centuries, down to the time of Peisistratus, and then for the first time reduced to writing. This shows at least what they have believed was possible. In Max Müller's "History of Ancient Sanskrit Literature" it is argued strongly that the Vedas were not written at first, but were transmitted orally, being learned by heart in the great religious schools of the Indo-Aryans as an indispensable part of education. This is likely to be true, whether we assume that the Indo-Aryans had or had not the art of writing; for, in the Vaidic age, the divine songs of the Veda were so intimately associated with the mysteries of their religion that they may have been held too sacred to be made common by written characters.

Therefore it is no wise incredible, nor even surprising, that a considerable amount of literature existed in Peru without the aid of writing. On the contrary, it would be surprising if they had failed to do what has been done by every other people in like circumstances. The schools of the *amautas* were national institutions specially set apart for the business of preserving and increasing knowledge, teaching, and literary work of every kind. In a country where civilization was so much advanced in many respects, they could not have been entirely barren. Those who criticise Montesinos admit that "his advantages were great," that "no one equaled him in archæological knowledge of Peru," and that "he became acquainted with original instruments which he occasionally transferred to his own pages, and which it would now be difficult to meet elsewhere." The results of his investigation are embodied in a work entitled "Memorias Antiguas Historiales del Peru." This, with another work on the Conquest entitled "Annales," remained in manuscript at Madrid until the "Memorias" was translated into French by M. Ternaux-Compans, and printed in his collection of original documents relating to the discovery and exploration of America.

HIS SCHEME OF PERUVIAN HISTORY.

According to Montesinos, there were three distinct periods in the history of Peru. First, there was a period which began with the origin of civilization, and lasted until the first or second century of the Christian era. Second, there was a period of disintegration, decline, and disorder, introduced by successful invasions from the east and southeast, during which the country was broken up into small states, and many of the arts of civilization were lost; this period lasted more than a thousand years. Third and last came the period of the Incas, who revived civilization and restored the empire. He discards the wonder-stories told of Manco-Capac and Mama Oello, and gives the Peruvian nation a beginning which is, at least, not incredible. It was originated, he says, by a people led by four brothers, who settled in the Valley of Cuzco, and developed civilization there in a very human way. The youngest of these brothers assumed supreme authority, and became the first of a long line of sovereigns.

Montesinos gives a list of sixty-four sovereigns who reigned in the first period. The first was Pûhua Manco, or Ayar-Uchu-Topa, the youngest of the four brothers, whose power was increased by the willing submission of "neighboring nations." His successor, called Manco-Capac, is described as a remarkable character; "adjacent nations dreaded his power," and in his time the kingdom was much increased. Next came Huainaevi-Pishua, and "during his reign was known the use of letters, and the *amautas* taught astrology and the art of writing on leaves of the plantain tree." Sinchi-Cozque won victories, and "adorned and fortified the city of Cuzco." Inti-Capac-Yupanqui, another remarkable character, divided the kingdom into districts and subdistricts, introduced a complete civil organization, instituted the solar year of three hundred and sixty-five days, and established the system of couriers. Manco-Capac II. "made great roads from Cuzco to the provinces." These are the first six rulers named on the list.

In the next thirteen reigns nothing special is noted save attention to civil affairs, occasional conquests, and "a great plague." The twentieth sovereign, called Huascar-Titupac, "gave all the provinces new governors of royal blood, and introduced in the army a cuirass made of cotton and copper." The twenty-first, Manco-Capac-Amauta, "being addicted to astronomy, convened a scientific council, which agreed that the sun was at a greater distance from the earth than the moon, and that they followed different courses." In the next twelve reigns, wars, conquests, and some indications of religious controversy are noted. The thirty-fourth ruler, called Ayay-Manco, "assembled the *amautas* in Cuzco to reform the calendar, and it was decided that the year should be divided into months of thirty days, and weeks of ten days, calling the five days at the end of the year a small week; they also collected the years into decades or groups of tens, and determined that each group of ten decades should form a sun."

Among the next twenty-nine sovereigns, Capac-Raymi-Amauta, the thirty-eighth of the line, and Yahuar-Huquiz, the fifty-first, were "celebrated for astronomical knowledge," and the latter "intercalated a year at the end of four centuries." Manco-Capac III., the sixtieth sovereign of this line, is supposed to have reigned at the beginning of the Christian era, and in his time "Peru had reached her greatest elevation and extension." The next three reigns covered thirty-two years, it is said. Then came Titu-Yupanqui-Pachacuti, the sixty-fourth and last sovereign of the old kingdom, who was killed in battle with a horde of invaders who came from the east and southeast across the Andes. His death threw the kingdom into confusion. There was rebellion as well as invasion, by which it was broken up into small states. The account of what happened says: "Many ambitious ones, taking advantage of the new king's youth, denied him obedience, drew away from him the people, and usurped several provinces. Those who remained faithful to the heir of Titu-Yupanqui conducted him to Tambotoco, whose inhabitants offered him obedience. From this it happened that this monarch took the title of King of Tambotoco."

During the next twenty-six reigns the sway of the old royal house was confined to this little state. These twenty-six successors of the old sovereigns were merely kings of Tambotoco. The country, overrun by rude invaders, torn by civil war, and harried by "many simultaneous tyrants," became semi-barbarous; "all was found in great confusion; life and personal safety were endangered, and civil disturbances caused an entire loss of the use of letters." The art of writing seems to have been mixed up with the issues of a religious controversy in the time of the old kingdom. It was proscribed now, even in the little state of Tambotoco, for we read that the fourteenth of its twenty-six rulers " prohibited, under the severest penalties, the use of *quellca* for writing, and forbade, also, the invention of letters. *Quellca* was a kind of parchment made of plantain leaves." It is added that an *amauta* who sought to restore the art of writing was put to death. This period of decline, disorder, and disintegration, which covered the "dark ages" of Peru, lasted until the rise of the Incas brought better times and reunited the country.

Rocca, called Inca-Rocca, was the first of the Incas. He was connected with the old royal family, but did not stand in the direct line of succession. The story of his rise to power is told as follows: "A princess of royal blood, named Mama-Ciboca, contrived, by artifice and intrigue, to raise to the throne her son called Rocca, a youth of twenty years, and so handsome and valiant that his admirers called him *Inca*, which means lord. This title of *Inca* began with him, and was adopted by all his successors." He appears to have had great qualities as a ruler. Not much time passed before he secured possession of Cuzco, made war successfully against the neighboring princes, and greatly extended his dominions. Under his successors, the empire thus begun continued to grow, until it was extended from Quito to Chili, and became the Peruvian empire which the Spaniards robbed and destroyed.

PROBABILITIES.

It has been the fashion to depreciate Montesinos, but I find it impossible to discover the reasons by which this depreciation can be justified. It is alleged that he uses fanciful hypotheses to explain Peru. The reply to this seems to me conclusive. In the first place, he is, in this respect, like all other writers of his time. That was an age of fanciful theories. Montesinos is certainly no worse than others in this respect, while he has the merit of being somewhat more original. He brought the Peruvian civilization from Armenia, and argued that Peru was Solomon's Ophir. Undue importance has been accorded to several of the old Spanish chroniclers, whose works contain suggestions and fancies much more irrational. In the second place, his theories have nothing whatever to do with his facts, by which they are sometimes contradicted. He found in Peru materials for the scheme of its ancient history, which he sets forth. Readers will form their own estimates of its value, but no reasonable critic will confound this part of his work with his fanciful explanations, which are sometimes inconsistent with it. For instance, his theory assumes that the first monarch of the old kingdom began his reign as far back in the past as the year 2500 B.C. But he reports only sixty-four rulers of that old kingdom. Now, if there were so many as sixty-four, and if we allow an average of twenty years to each reign (which is sufficient), we can not carry back the beginning of that first reign to the year 1200 B.C.

There is another objection, which must be stated in the words of one of the critics who have urged it: "Montesinos treats the ancient history of Peru in a mode so original and distinct from all others that we can perceive it to be a production alike novel and unknown." If this means any thing, it means that it was highly improper for Montesinos to find in Peru what was "unknown" to poorly-informed and superficial Spanish writers, who had already been accepted as "authorities." It would have been singular if his careful investigation, continued through fifteen years, had not given him a great amount of information which others had never taken pains to acquire. His treatment of the subject was "original and distinct from all others," because he knew what other writers did not know. His information did not allow him to repeat the marvelous story of Manco-Capac and Mama Oello, nor to confine Peruvian history to the time of the Incas. But when the result of his inquiries was announced in Europe, Garcilasso and others regulated the fashion of Peruvian studies, and the influence of their limited and superficial knowledge of the subject has been felt ever since.

The curious theories of Montesinos may be brushed aside as rubbish, or be studied with other vagaries of that age in order to understand its difference from ours; but whoever undertakes to criticise his facts needs to be his equal in knowledge of Peru. His works, however, tell us all that can ever be known of Peruvian ancient history, for the facilities for investigation which existed in his time are no longer possible. It may, however, be useful to consider that the main fact in his report on the subject is no more "original and distinct" than the testimony of the monuments around Lake Titicaca. The significance of this testimony is now generally admitted. There *was* a period in the history of Peruvian civilization much earlier than that of the Incas, a period still represented by these old monuments which, so far as relates to this point, are as "novel" and "original" as Montesinos himself.

That the civilization found in the country was much older than the Incas can be seen in what we know of their history. Their empire had grown to be what Pizarro found it by subjugating and absorbing a considerable number of small states, which had existed as civilized states before their time. The conquest of Quito, which was not inferior to the Valley of Cuzco in civilization, had just been completed when the Spaniards arrived. The Chimus, subjugated a few years earlier, are described as even more advanced in civilization than any other Peruvian community. The small states thus absorbed by Peru were much alike in manners, customs, manufactures, methods of building, and general culture. It is manifest that their civilization had a common origin, and that to find its origin we must go back into the past far beyond Inca-Rocco, the first of his line, who began the work of uniting them under one government.

Moreover, there were civilized communities in that

part of the continent which the Incas had not subjugated, such as the Muyscas on the table-land of Bogota, north of Quito, who had a remarkable civil and religious organization, a temple of the sun built with stone columns, a regular system of computing time, a peculiar calendar, and who used small circular gold plates as coin. They were described by Humboldt.

The condition of the people composing the Peruvian empire at the time of the Conquest bore witness to an ancient history something like that reported by Montesinos. There were indications that the country had undergone important revolutionary changes before this empire was established. The Peruvians at that time were not all one people. The political union was complete, but there were differences of speech, and, to some extent, of physical characteristics. Three numerous and important branches of the population were known as Aymaraes, Chinchas, and Huancas. They used different tongues, although the Quichua dialect, spoken by the Incas, and doubtless a dialect of the Aymaraes, to whom the Incas belonged, was the official language in every part of the empire. There was a separated and fragmentary condition of the communities with respect to their unlike characteristics, which implied something different from a quiet and uniform political history. These differences and peculiarities suggest that there was a period when Peru, after an important career of civilization and empire, was subjected to great political changes brought about by invasion and revolution, by which the nation was for a long time broken up into separate states.

Here, as in Mexico and Central America, there was in the traditions frequent mention of strangers or foreigners who came by sea to the Pacific coast and held intercourse with the people; but this was in the time of the old kingdom. As the Malays and other island people under their influence formerly traversed the Pacific, this is not improbable. Some have assumed that the Peruvians had no communication with the Mexicans and Central Americans, and that the two peoples were unknown to each other. This, however, seems to be contradicted by the fact that an accurate knowledge of Peru was found among the people inhabiting the Isthmus and the region north of it. The Spaniards heard of Peru on the Atlantic coast of South America, but on the Isthmus Balboa gained clear information in regard to that country from natives who had evidently seen it. To what extent there was intercourse between the two civilized portions of the continent is unknown. They had vessels quite as good as most of those constructed at Panama by the Spanish hunters for Peru, such as the *balsas* of the Peruvians and the "shallop" of the Mayas seen by Columbus, which made communication possible up and down the coast; but whether regular intercourse between them was ever established, and every thing else relating to this matter, must necessarily be left to a calculation of probabilities.

CONCLUSION.

If, as seems most likely, there was in South America an ancient development of civilized human life, out of which arose the civilizations found in Peru and Central America, its antiquity was much greater than can be comprehended by the current chronologies. This, however, can not make it improbable, for these chronologies are really no more reasonable than the monkish fancies used in the sixteenth and seventeenth centuries to explain these civilizations. We find the hagiologists very absurd, but the condition of mind which made them possible is closely akin to that which moves some men in our time to deny or limit the past, and reject the results of any investigation which tend to enlarge it. Rational inquiry constantly forces upon us the suggestion that there was more in the unwritten history of the human race than our inherited modes of thinking have allowed us to suppose, and that the beginning of civilization is far more ancient than our long accepted theories of antiquity are able to admit.

What may be discovered in South America by a more complete geological and palæontological investigation it is not now possible to say. Professor Orton, in his recent book, "The Andes and the Amazon," far exceeds Montesinos in his estimate of the antiquity of Peruvian civilization. He says on this point:

"Geology and archæology are combining to prove that Sorato and Chimborazo have looked down upon a civilization far more ancient than that of the Incas, and perhaps coeval with the flint-flakes of Cornwall and the shell-mounds of Denmark. On the shores of Lake Titicaca are extensive ruins which antedate the advent of Manco-Capac, and may be as venerable as the lake-dwellings of Geneva. Wilson has traced six terraces in going up from the sea through the province of Esmeraldas toward Quito, and underneath the living forest, which is older than the Spanish invasion, many gold, copper, and stone vestiges of a lost population were found. In all cases these relics are situated below the high-tide mark, in a bed of marine sediment, from which he infers that this part of the country formerly stood higher above the sea. If this be true, vast must be the antiquity of these remains, for the upheaval and subsidence of the coast is exceedingly slow."—P. 109.

This refers to discoveries made on the coast of Ecuador in 1860, by James S. Wilson, Esq. At various points along this coast he found "ancient or fossil pottery, vessels, images," and other manufactured articles, all finely wrought. Some of these articles were made of gold. The most remarkable fact connected with them is that they were taken from "a stratum of ancient surface earth" which was covered with a marine deposit six feet thick. The geological formation where these remains were found is reported to be "as old as the drift strata of Europe," and "identical with that of Guayaquil in which bones of the mastodon are met with." The ancient surface earth or vegetable mould, with its pottery, gold-work, and other relics of civilized human life, was, therefore, below the sea when that marine deposit was spread over it. This land, after being occupied by men, had subsided and settled below the ocean, remained there long enough to accumulate the marine deposit, and again been elevated to its former position above the sea level.

Since this elevation, forests have been established over it which are older than the Spanish Conquest, and now it is once more subsiding. In 1862, at a meeting of the Royal Geological Society, Sir Roderick Murchison spoke of these discoveries as follows:

"The discoveries Mr. Wilson has made of the existence of the works of man in a stratum of mould beneath the sea level, and covered by several feet of clay, the phenomenon being persistent for sixty miles, are of the highest interest to physical geographers and geologists. The facts seem to demonstrate that, within the human period, the lands on the west coast of Equatorial America were depressed and submerged, and that after the accumulation of marine clays above the terrestrial relics the whole coast was elevated to its present position."

Assuming the facts to be as Mr. Wilson reports (and they have not been called in question), it follows that there was human civilization to a certain extent in South America at the time of the older stone age of Western Europe. The oldest Peruvian date of Montesinos is quite modern compared with this. The fact may be considered in connection with another mentioned in the section on American Ethnology, namely, that the most ancient fauna on this continent, man probably included, is that of South America. But, without regard to what may be signified by these discoveries of Mr. Wilson, there is good reason for believing that the Peruvian civilization was much more ancient than it has been the fashion to admit.

Peru would now be a very different country if the

Spaniards had been sufficiently controlled by Christianity and civilization to treat the Peruvians justly, and seek nothing more than friendly intercourse with them. But they went there as greedy buccaneers, unscrupulous robbers, and brought every thing to ruin. At no time since the Spanish Conquest has the country been as orderly, as prosperous, or as populous as they found it. It has fallen to a much lower condition. Industry and thrift have been supplanted by laziness and beggarly poverty. Ignorance and incapacity have taken the place of that intelligence and enterprise which enabled the old Peruvians to maintain their remarkable system of agriculture, complete their great works, and made them so industrious and skillful in their manufactures. The region covered by the Peruvian empire has not half as many people now as it had in the time of the Incas. Is it possible to imagine the present inhabitants of Ecuador, Peru, and Bolivia cultivating their soil with intelligent industry, building aqueducts five hundred miles long, and constructing magnificently paved roads through the rocks and across the ravines of the Andes, from Quito to Chili? One of the scholars connected with the scientific expedition which visited South America in 1867, describing the ancient greatness and present inferior condition of Quito, exclaims, "May the future bring it days equal to those when it was called the 'City of the Incas!'" He might appropriately utter a similar wish for the whole country.

APPENDIX.

APPENDIX.

A.

THE NORTHMEN IN AMERICA.

It is generally known, I suppose, that original manuscript records of Norse voyages to this continent have been carefully preserved in Iceland, and that they were first published at Copenhagen in 1837, with a Danish and a Latin translation. These narratives are plain, straightforward, business-like accounts of actual voyages made by the Northmen, in the tenth and eleventh centuries, to Greenland, Newfoundland, Nova Scotia, and the coast of Massachusetts and Rhode Island. Within the whole range of the literature of discovery and adventure no volumes can be found which have more abundant internal evidence of authenticity. It always happens, when something important is unexpectedly added to our knowledge of the past, that somebody will blindly disbelieve. Dugald Stewart could see nothing but "frauds of arch-forgers" in what was added to our knowledge of ancient India when the Sanskrit language and literature were discovered. In the same way, here and there a doubter has hesitated to accept the fact communicated by these Norse records; but, with the evidence before us, we may as reasonably doubt any unquestioned fact of history which depends on similar testimony.

Any account of these voyages should be prefaced by some notice of Iceland. Look on a map at the position of Iceland, and you will see at once that it should not be classed as a European island. It belongs to North America. It was, in fact, unknown to modern Europe until the year 861 A.D., when it was discovered by Nadodd, a Norse rover. There is some reason to believe the Irish had previously sailed to this island, but no settlement was established in it previous to the year 875, when it was occupied by a colony of Norwegians under a chief named Ingolf. Owing to civil troubles in Norway, he was soon followed by many of the most intelligent, wealthy, and honorable of his countrymen.

Thus Iceland, away in the Northern Ocean, became a place of great interest. In the tenth and eleventh centuries the Icelanders had become eminent among the Norse communities for intellectual culture and accomplishment. They were far superior to their countrymen in Norway. To them we are indebted for the existing records of Scandinavian mythology. They were daring and adventurous navigators, and, when we consider how near Iceland is to America, it should not surprise us to hear that they found the American continent; on the contrary, it would have been surprising if they had failed to find it. They first discovered Greenland, and in 982 established a colony there. Afterward, in the course of many voyages, they explored the coast of America much farther south.

Narratives of some of these voyages were carefully written and preserved. There are two principal records. One is entitled "An Account of Eirek the Red and Greenland." This appears to have been written in Greenland, where Eirek settled, and where the Northmen had a colony consisting of two hundred and eighty settlements. The other record is an "Account of Thorfinn Karlsefne." This was written in Iceland by a bishop, one of Thorfinn's immediate descendants. The Norse narrative introduces Eirek's voyage of discovery as follows:

"There was a man of noble family, whose name was Thorvald. He and his son Eirek, surnamed the Red, were obliged to flee from Jadir (in the southwest part of Norway) because, in some feud that arose, they committed a homicide. They went to Iceland, which, at that time, was thoroughly colonized."

Thorvald died soon after reaching Iceland, but Eirek inherited his restless spirit. The record says he was at length involved in another feud in Iceland. Eirek, being unjustly treated by some of his neighbors, committed another homicide, and the narrative relates what followed: "Having been condemned by the court, he resolved to leave Iceland. His vessel being prepared, and every thing ready, Eirek's partisans in the quarrel accompanied him some distance. He told them he had determined to quit Iceland and settle somewhere else, adding that he was going in search of the land Gunnibern had seen when driven by a storm into the Western Ocean, and promising to revisit them if his search should be successful. Sailing from the western side of Iceland, Eirek steered boldly to the west. At length he found land, and called the place Midjokul. Then, coasting along the shore in a southerly direction, he sought to find a place more suitable for settlement. He spent the winter on a part of the coast which he named "Eirek's Island." A satisfactory situation for his colony was found, and he remained there two years.

On returning to Iceland he called the discovered country "Greenland," saying to his confidential friends, "A name so inviting will induce men to emigrate thither." Finally, he went again to Greenland, accompanied by "twenty-five ships" filled with emigrants and stores, and his colony was established. "This happened," says the chronicle, "fifteen winters before the Christian religion was introduced into Iceland;" that is to say, Eirek made this second voyage to Greenland fifteen years previous to 1000 A.D. Biarni, son of Heriulf, a chief man among these colonists, was absent in Norway when his father left Iceland. On returning, he decided to follow and join the colony, although neither he nor any of his companions had ever seen Greenland, or sailed on the "Greenland Ocean." Having arranged his business, he set sail, and made one of the most remarkable and fearful voyages on record.

On leaving Iceland they sailed three days with a fair wind; then arose a storm of northeasterly winds, accompanied by very cloudy, thick weather. They were driven before this storm for many days, they knew not whither. At length the weather cleared, and they could see the sky. Then they sailed west another day, and saw land different from any they had previously known, for it "was not mountainous." In reply to the anxious sailors, Biarni said this could not be Greenland. They put the ship about and steered in a northeasterly direction two days more. Again they saw land which was low and level. Biarni thought this could not be Greenland. For three more days they sailed in the same direction, and came to a land that was "mountainous, and covered with ice." This proved to be an island, around which they sailed. Steering toward the north, they sailed four days and again discovered land, which Biarni thought was Greenland, and so it proved. They were on the southern coast, near the new settlement.

It is manifest that the first land Biarni saw was either Nantucket or Cape Cod; the next was Nova Scotia, around Cape Sable; and the island around which they coasted was Newfoundland. This voyage was made five hundred and seven years earlier than the first voyage of Columbus.

Biarni's report of his discoveries was heard with great interest, and caused much speculation; but the settlers in Greenland were too busy making their new homes to undertake voyages in that direction immediately. Fourteen years later, Leif, a son of Eirek the Red, being in Norway, was incited to fit out an expedition to go in search of the strange lands Biarni had seen. On returning to Greenland "he had an interview with Biarni, and bought his ship, which he fitted out and manned with thirty-five men." The first land seen by Leif, after he sailed from Greenland, was the island around which Biarni sailed. This he named Helluland (the land of broad stones). Sailing on toward the south, they came next to a land that was low and level, and covered with wood. This they called Markland (the land of woods). The narrative goes on; "They now put to sea with a northeast wind, and, sailing still toward the south, after two days touched at an island [Nantucket?] which lay opposite the northeast part of the main land." Then they "sailed through a bay between this island and a cape running northeast, and, going westward, sailed past the Cape;" and at length they "passed up a river into a bay," where they landed. They had probably reached Mount Hope Bay.

They constructed rude dwellings, and prepared to spend the winter at this place. It was about mid-autumn, and, finding wild grapes, they called the country Vinland. Leif and his people were much pleased with "the mildness of the climate and goodness of the soil." The next spring they loaded their vessels with timber and returned to Greenland, where, Eirek the Red having died, Leif inherited his estate and authority, and left exploring expeditions to others.

The next year Leif's brother Thorvald went to Vinland with one ship and thirty men, and there passed the winter. The following summer he explored the coast westward and southward, and seems to have gone as far south as the Carolinas. In the autumn they returned to Vinland, where they passed another winter. The next summer they coasted around Cape Cod toward Boston Harbor, and, getting aground on Cape Cod, they called it *Kialarness*, Keel Cape. Here the chronicle first speaks of the natives, whom it calls "Skraellings." It says: "They perceived on the sandy shore of the bay three small elevations. On going to them they found three boats made of skins, and under each boat three men. They seized all the men but one, who was so nimble as to escape with his boat;" and "*they killed all those whom they had taken.*" The doctrine of "natural enemies" was more current among the old Northmen than that of human brotherhood.

A retribution followed swiftly. They were presently attacked by a swarm of natives in boats. The "Skraellings" were beaten off; but Thorvald, being fatally wounded in the skirmish, died, and was buried on a neighboring promontory. His companions, after passing a third winter in Vinland, returned to Greenland, having been absent three years. This, considering the circumstances, was an adventurous voyage, a brave exploring expedition sent from the arctic regions to make discoveries in the mysterious world at the south. On reading the narrative, one longs for that more ample account of the voyage which would have been given if Thorvald himself had lived to return.

The "Account of Eirek the Red and Greenland" tells of an expedition planned by Eirek's youngest son, Thorstein, which was prevented by Thorstein's death. It relates the particulars of a voyage to Vinland made by Eirek's daughter, Freydis, with her husband and his two brothers. Freydis is described as a cruel, hard-hearted, enterprising woman, "mindful only of gain." The chronicle says her husband, named Thorvald, was "weak-minded," and that she married him because he was rich. During the voyage she contrived to destroy her husband's brothers and seize their ship, for which evil deed she was made to feel her brother Leif's anger on her return. The same chronicle gives an account of a voyage northward, up Baffin's Bay, and through what is now called Wellington Channel. There is also a romantic story of Thorstein's widow, Gudrid, an exceedingly beautiful and noble-minded woman, which tells how she was courted and married by Thorfinn Karlsefne, a man of distinguished character and rank, who came from Iceland with ships, and was entertained by Leif.

Thorfinn came to Greenland in the year 1006, and, having married Gudrid, Thorstein's widow, was induced by her to undertake a voyage to Vinland. They left Greenland with three ships and a hundred and sixty men, taking with them livestock and all things necessary to the establishment of a colony. The vessels touched at Newfoundland and Nova Scotia, and, having reached Vinland, they passed up Buzzard's Bay, disembarked their livestock, and preparations were made for winter residence. Here they passed the winter; and here Gudrid gave birth to a son, who lived and grew to manhood, and among whose lineal descendants was Thorvaldsen, the Danish sculptor.

The winter was severe; their provisions began to fail, and they were threatened with famine. This occasioned many anxieties and some adventures. One of the company, a fierce, resolute man, bewailed their apostasy from the old religion, and declared that to find relief they must return to the worship of Thor. But they found a supply of provisions without trying this experiment. Thor's worshiper afterward left the company with a few companions to pursue an expedition of his own, and was killed by the natives.

The next spring Thorfinn explored the coast farther west and south. Then he went to the bay where Leif spent the winter, and there passed his second winter in Vinland. He called the bay Hóp. The Indians called it Haup; we call it Hope. During the next season they saw many natives and had much intercourse with them, which finally led to hostilities. The natives, in great numbers, attacked them fiercely, but were signally defeated. Freydis, being with the company, fought desperately in this battle, and greatly distinguished herself as a terrible combatant, although in that peculiar condition which does not specially qualify a woman for such exploits. Thorfinn afterward explored Massachusetts Bay, spent a third winter in Vinland, and then, with part of the company, returned to Greenland. He finally went back to his home in Iceland, and there remained during the rest of his life.

The Indians had traditions which appear to have preserved recollections of these visits of the Northmen. In 1787, Michael Lort, Vice-president of the London Antiquarian Society, published a work, in which he quoted the following extract of a letter from New England, dated more than half a century earlier: "There was a tradition current with the oldest Indians in these parts that there came a wooden house, and men of another country in it, swimming up the Assoonet, as this (Taunton) river was then called, who fought the Indians with mighty success."

There was now a settlement in Vinland, at Hóp Bay, and voyages to that region became frequent. The old Norse narrative says: "Expeditions to Vinland now became very frequent matters of consideration, for these expeditions were considered both lucrative and honorable." The following appears in Wheaton's History of the Northmen: "A part of Thorfinn's company remained in Vinland, and were afterward joined by two Icelandic chieftains. * * In the year 1059, it is said, an Irish or Saxon priest named Jon or John, who had spent some time in Iceland, went to preach to the colonists in Vinland, where he was murdered by the heathen." The following is from the Introduction to Henderson's Iceland: "In the year 1121, Eirck, bishop of Greenland, made a voyage to Vinland."

Thus it appears to be an authenticated fact that the Northmen had a settlement or settlements in New England six hundred years previous to the arrival of English settlers. It is probable that their Vinland settlements consisted chiefly of trading and lumbering establishments. The first explorers "loaded their vessels with timber" when ready to return to Greenland, where the lack of timber was so great that the settlers found it necessary to use stone for building material. The Vinland timber-trade became naturally an important business, but neither Greenland nor Iceland could furnish emigrants to occupy the country. Traces of the old Norse settlements in Greenland are still visible in the ruins of stone buildings. Near the Bay of Igalito, in Greenland, are remains of a stone church. Vinland was covered with great forests, and there it was much easier and cheaper to build houses of wood.

The Norse records speak also of a region south of Vinland to which voyages were made. It is called Huitramannaland. Indeed, two great regions farther south are mentioned. There is a romantic story of one Biorn Asbrandson, a noble Icelander, who, being crossed in his matrimonial desires, went away toward Vinland; but his vessel was driven much farther south by a storm. Nothing was heard of him until part of the crew of a Norse vessel, on a voyage to Huitramannaland, were captured by the natives, among whom Biorn was living as a chief. He discovered an old acquaintance among the prisoners whom he found means to release. He talked freely with his old friend of the past, and of Iceland, but would not leave his savage friends.

How little we know of what has been in the past ages, notwithstanding our many volumes of history! We listen attentively to what gets a wide and brilliant publication, and either fail to hear or doubt every thing else. If these Norse adventurers had sailed from England or Spain, those countries being what they were in the time of Columbus, their colonies would not have failed, through lack of men and means to support and extend them, and the story of their discoveries would have been told in every language and community of the civilized world. But the little communities in Iceland and Greenland were very different from rich and powerful nations. Instead of being in direct communication with the great movements of human life in Europe, recorded in what we read as history, they were far off in the Northern Ocean, and, out of Norway, almost unknown to Europe. Afterward, when the name and discoveries of Columbus had taken control of thought and imagination, it became difficult for even intelligent men, with the old Norse records before them, to see the claims of the Northmen.

B.

THE WELSH IN AMERICA.

THE story of the emigration to America of Prince Madoc, or Madog, is told in the old Welsh books as follows:

About the year 1168 or 1169 A.D., Owen Gwynedd, ruling prince of North Wales, died, and among his sons there was a contest for the succession, which, becoming angry and fierce, produced a civil war. His son Madoc, who had "command of the fleet," took no part in this strife. Greatly disturbed by the public trouble, and not being able to make the combatants hear reason, he resolved to leave Wales and go across the ocean to the land at the west. Accordingly, in the year 1170 A.D., he left with a few ships, going south of Ireland, and steering westward. The purpose of this voyage was to explore the western land and select a place for settlement. He found a pleasant and fertile region, where his settlement was established. Leaving one hundred and twenty persons, he returned to Wales, prepared ten ships, prevailed on a large company, some of whom were Irish, to join him, and sailed again to America. Nothing more was ever heard in Wales of Prince Madog or his settlement.

All this is related in old Welsh annals preserved in the abbeys of Conway and Strat Flur. These annals were used by Humphrey Llwyd in his translation and continuation of Caradoc's History of Wales, the continuation extending from 1157 to 1270 A.D. This emigration of Prince Madog is mentioned in the preserved works of several Welsh bards who lived before the time of Columbus. It is mentioned by Hakluyt, who had his account of it from writings of the bard Guttun Owen. As the Northmen had been in New England over one hundred and fifty years when Prince Madog went forth to select a place for his settlement, he knew very well there was a continent on the other side of the Atlantic, for he had knowledge of their voyages to America; and knowledge of them was also prevalent in Ireland. His emigration took place when Henry II. was king of England, but in that age the English knew little or nothing of Welsh affairs in such a way as to connect them with English history very closely.

It is supposed that Madog settled somewhere in the Carolinas, and that his colony, unsupported by new arrivals from Europe, and cut off from communication with that side of the ocean, became weak, and, after being much reduced, was destroyed or absorbed by some powerful tribe of Indians. In our colony times, and later, there was no lack of reports that relics of Madog's Welshmen, and even their language, had been discovered among the Indians; but generally they were entitled to no credit. The only report of this kind having any show of claim to respectful consideration is that of Rev. Morgan Jones, made in 1686, in a letter giving an account of his adventures among the Tuscaroras. These Tuscarora Indians were lighter in color than the other tribes, and this peculiarity was so noticeable that they were frequently mentioned as "White Indians." Mr. Jones's account of his experiences among them was written in March, 1686, and published in the Gentleman's Magazine for the year 1740, as follows:

"REV. MORGAN JONES'S STATEMENT.

"These presents certify all persons whatever, that in the year 1660, being an inhabitant of Virginia, and chaplain to Major General Bennet, of Manwoman County, the said Major General Bennet and Sir William Berkeley sent two ships to Port Royal, now called South Carolina, which is sixty leagues southward of Cape Fair, and I was sent therewith to be their minister. Upon the 8th of April we set out from Virginia, and arrived at the harbor's mouth of Port Royal the 19th of the same month, where we waited for the rest of the fleet that was to sail from Barbadoes and Bermuda with one Mr. West, who was to be deputy governor of said place. As soon as the fleet came in, the smallest vessels that were with us sailed up the river to a place called the Oyster Point; there I continued about eight months, all which time being almost starved for want of provisions: I and five more traveled through the wilderness till we came to the Tuscarora country.

"There the Tuscarora Indians took us prisoners because we told them that we were bound to Roanock. That night they carried us to their town and shut us up close, to our no small dread. The next day they entered into a consultation about us, and, after it was over, their interpreter told us that we must prepare ourselves to die next morning, whereupon, being very much dejected, I spoke to this effect in the British [Welsh] tongue: 'Have I escaped so many dangers, and must I now be knocked on the head like a dog!' Then presently came an Indian to me, which afterward appeared to be a war captain belonging to the sachem of the Doegs (whose original, I find, must needs be from the Old Britons), and took me up by the middle, and told me in the British [Welsh] tongue I should not die, and thereupon went to the emperor of Tuscarora, and agreed for my ransom and the men that were with me.

"They (the Doegs) then welcomed us to their town, and entertained us very civilly and cordially four months, during which time I had the opportunity of conversing with them familiarly in the British [Welsh] language, and did preach to them in the same language three times a week, and they would confer with me about any thing that was difficult therein, and at our departure they abundantly supplied us with whatever was necessary to our support and well doing. They are settled upon Pontigo River, not far from Cape Atros. This is a brief recital of my travels among the Doeg Indians. MORGAN JONES,

"the son of John Jones, of Basateg, near Newport, in the County of Monmouth. I am ready to conduct any Welshman or others to the country.

"New York, March 10th, 1685-6."

Other accounts of his "travels" among the "Doegs" of the Tuscarora nation were published much earlier, but no other has been preserved. His veracity was never questioned. What shall be said of his statement? Were the remains of Prince Madog's company represented in these "Doeg" Tuscaroras? He is very explicit in regard to the matter of language, and it is not easy to see how he could be mistaken. They understood his Welsh, not without needing explanation of some things "difficult therein." He was able to converse with them and preach to them in Welsh; and yet, if he got an explanation of the existence of the Welsh language among these "Doegs," or sought to know any thing in regard to their traditional history, he omits entirely to say so. Without meaning to doubt his veracity, one feels skeptical, and desires a more intelligent and complete account of these "travels."

C.

ANTIQUITIES OF THE PACIFIC ISLANDS.

There are indications that the Pacific world had an important ancient history, and these multiply as our knowledge of that world increases. The wide diffusion of Malay dialects in the Pacific Islands suggests the controlling influence by which that ancient history was directed. The ancient remains at Easter Island are known; two of the "great images" found there are now in the British Museum. All who have examined this island believe these remains "were the work of a former race," and that it had formerly "an abundant population." It is not generally known that antiquities more important than these exist on many of the other islands of the Pacific Ocean.

An educated and very intelligent gentleman, who has lived many years on one of these islands, and visited a considerable portion of Polynesia, finds that the Pacific has antiquities which deserve attention. He has sent me papers containing descriptions of some of them, taken from the diary of an intelligent and observant shipmaster, much of whose life as a mariner has been passed on the Pacific. These papers were prepared for publication in a newspaper at Sydney. The gentleman sending them says in his letter: "These researches are not very minute or accurate, but they indicate that there is a vast field ready for exploration in the Pacific, as well as in Central America and Egypt."

The papers to which I refer begin with ruins observed in the island of Ascension or Fanipe, and describe "the great temple" at Metallanine. This was a large edifice, well built of stone, and connected with canals and earth-works. "Vaults, passages, and platforms, all of basaltic stones," are mentioned; also, "below the pavement of the main quadrangle, on opposite sides, are two passages or gateways, each about ten feet square, pierced through the outer wall down to the waters of the canal." Within the walls is a "central pyramidal chamber or temple," with a tree growing on it. The whole ruin is now covered with trees and other vegetation.

Other ruins exist in the island, one or two of which are described. "Some are close upon the sea-shore, others are on the tops of solitary hills, and some are found on plateaus or cleared spaces far inland, but commanding views of the sea. One of the latter kind is a congeries of ruinous heaps of square stones, covering at least five or six acres. It is situated on a piece of table-land, surrounded by dense forest growths, and itself covered with low jungle. There is the appearance of a ditch, in the form of a cross, at the intersecting angles of which are tall mounds of ruin, of which the original form is now undistinguishable beyond the fact that the basements, constructed of large stones, indicate that the structures were square. The natives can not be induced to go near this place, although it abounds in wild pigeons, which they are extremely fond of hunting."

These ruined structures were not built by barbarous people such as now inhabit the island of Ascension. There is no tradition relating to their origin or history among the present inhabitants, who, it is said, attribute them to "mauli," evil spirits. The "great temple" was occupied for a time, "several generations ago," according to the natives, by the shipwrecked crew of a Spanish buccaneer; and relics of these outlaws are still found in its vaults, which they used as storehouses.

On many low islands of the Marshall and Gilbert groups are curious pyramids, tall and slender, built of stones. The natives regard them with superstitious fear. The author of these papers, being a mariner, suggests that they are "landmarks or relics of ancient copper-colored voyagers of the Polynesian race during their great migrations." Remarkable structures of this kind are found on Tapituea, one of the Kingsmill islands, and on Tinian, one of the Ladrones, where, also, remarkable Cyclopean structures are found. They are solid, truncated pyramidal columns, generally about twenty feet high and ten feet square at the base. The monuments on Tinian were seen by M. Arago, who accompanied Bougainville. According to his description they form two long colonnades, the two rows being thirty feet apart, and seeming to have once been connected by something like roofing. On Swallow's Island, some twelve degrees eastward of Tapituea, is a pyramid similar in construction; and on the west side of this island is "a vast quadrangular inclosure of stone, containing several mounds, or probably edifices of some kind, of which the form and contents are not known by reason of their being buried under drift-sand and guano."

On Strong's Island, and others connected with it, are ruins similar to those at Metallanime. On Lele, which is separated from Strong's Island at the harbor by a very narrow channel, there is a "conical mountain surrounded by a wall some twenty feet high, and of enormous thickness." The whole island appears to present "a series of Cyclopean inclosures and lines of great walls every where overgrown with forest." Some of the inclosures are parallelograms 200 by 100 feet in extent; one is much larger. The walls are generally twelve feet thick, and within are vaults, artificial caverns, and secret passages. No white man is allowed to live on Lele, and strangers are forbidden to examine the ruins, in which, it is supposed, is concealed the plunder taken by the natives from captured or stranded ships. On the southwest side of the harbor, at Strong's Island, "are many canals lined with stone. They cross each other at right angles, and the islands between their intersections were artificially raised, and had tall buildings erected on them, some of which are still entire. One quadrangular tower, about forty feet high, is very remarkable. The forest around them is dense and gloomy; the canals are broken and choked with mangroves." Not more than 500 people now inhabit these islands; their tradition is, that an ancient city formerly stood around this harbor, mostly on Lele, occupied by a powerful people whom they call "Anut," and who had large vessels, in which they made long voyages east and west, "many moons" being required for one of these voyages.

Great stone structures on some of Navigator's Islands, of which the natives can give no account, are mentioned without being particularly described. Some account is given of one remarkable structure. On a mountain ridge 1500 feet above the sea, and near the edge of a precipice 500 feet high, is a circular platform built of huge blocks of volcanic stone. It is 150 feet in diameter, and about 20 feet high. On one side was the precipice, and on the other a ditch that may have been originally 20 feet deep. Trees six feet in diameter are now growing in the ruins of this platform. Remarkable ruins exist on some of the Marquesas Islands, but they have not been clearly described.

At first, when these antiquities were noticed by seamen, it was suggested that they were the remains of works constructed by the old buccaneers; but closer examination soon put aside this theory. Neither the buccaneers, nor any other people from Europe, would have constructed such works; and, besides, it is manifest that they were ruins before any crew of buccaneers sailed on the Pacific. The remains on Easter Island were described by Captain Cook. It has now been discovered that such remains exist at various points throughout Polynesia, and greater familiarity with the islands will very likely bring to light many that have not yet been seen by Europeans. The author of these papers, referring to the old discarded suggestion relative to the buccaneers, says: "Centuries of European occupation would have been required for the existence of such extensive remains, which are, moreover, not in any style of architecture practiced by people of the Old World."

It is stated that similar stone-work, consisting of "walls, strongholds, and great inclosures," exists on the eastern side of Formosa, which is occupied by a people wholly distinct in race from the Mongols who invaded and occupied the other side. The influence to which these ancient works are due seems to have pervaded Polynesia from the Marquesas Islands at the east, to the Ladrone and Carolina Islands at the west, and what is said of the present inhabitants of Ascension Island might have a wider application, namely, "They create on the mind of a stranger the impression of a people who have degenerated from something higher and better." At a few points in Polynesia a small portion of the people show Mongol traits. Dark-colored people, evidently of the Papuan variety, somewhat mixed with the brown race it may be, are found at various points in larger numbers; but the great body of the Polynesians are a brown race, established (at a very remote period, perhaps) by a mixture of the Papuans with the Malays. Now take into consideration the former existence of a great Malayan empire, the wide distribution of Malay dialects on the Pacific, and the various indications that there was formerly in Polynesia something higher and better in the condition of the people, and the ancient history indicated by these ruins will not seem mysterious, nor shall we feel constrained to treat as incredible the Central American and Peruvian traditions that anciently strangers came from the Pacific world in ships to the west coast of America for commercial intercourse with the civilized countries existing here.

Ruins similar in character are found in the Sandwich Islands, but here the masonry is occasionally superior to that found elsewhere. A gentleman interested in archæological inquiries gives the following account of a Hawaiian ruin which he visited in the interior, about thirty miles from Hilo. He says he went with several companions to the hill of Kukii, which he describes as follows:

"The hill is so regular in its outline that it appears like a work of art, a giant effort of the Mound-Builders. Its general form resembles very much the pyramid of Cholula in Mexico, and from this fact I felt a great interest in climbing it. We proceeded, Conway, Eldhardt, Kaiser, and I, on foot up the grassy slope of the hill. There was an absence of all volcanic matter; no stone on the hill except what had been brought there by the hand of man. As we arrived near the summit we came upon great square blocks of hewn stone overgrown by shrubbery, and on reaching the summit we found that it had been leveled and squared according to the cardinal points, and paved. We found two square blocks of hewn stone imbedded in the earth in an upright position, some fifteen feet apart, and ranging exactly east and west. Over the platform was rank grass, and a grove of cocoanuts some hundred years old. Examining farther, I found that the upper portion of the hill had been terraced; the terraces near the summit could be distinctly traced, and they had evidently been faced with hewn stone. The stones were in perfect squares of not less than three feet in diameter, many of them of much greater size. They were composed of a dark vitreous basalt, the most durable of all stone. It is remarkable that every slab was faced and polished upon every side, so that they could fit together like sheets of paper. They reminded me much of the polished stones in some of the walls of Tiahuanaco, and other ruins in Peru. Many of the blocks were lying detached; probably some had been removed; but there were still some thirty feet of the facing on the lower terrace partly in position. But all showed the ravages of time and earthquakes, and were covered with accumulated soil, grass, and shrubbery. Conway and myself, in descending the hill, had our attention attracted by a direct line of shrubbery running from the summit to the base of the hill, on the western side, to the cocoanut grove below. Upon examination, we found it to be the remains of a stairway, evidently of hewn stone, that had led from the foot of the hill to the first terrace, a height of nearly 300 feet. Within this stairway, near the base, we found a cocoanut-tree growing, more than 200 years old, the roots pressing out the rocks. The site for a temple is grand and imposing, and the view extensive, sweeping the ocean, the mountains, and the great lava plain of Puna. It was also excellent in a military point of view as a lookout. From the summit it appeared as an ancient green island, around which had surged and rolled a sea of lava; and so it evidently has been.

"By whom and when was this hill terraced and these stones hewn? There is a mystery hanging around this hill which exists nowhere else in the Sandwich Islands. The other structures so numerously scattered over the group are made of rough stone; there is no attempt at a terrace; there is no flight of steps leading to them; there is no hewn or polished stone, nor is there any evidence of the same architectural skill evinced. They are the oldest ruins yet discovered, and were evidently erected by a people considerably advanced in arts, acquainted with the use of metallic instruments, the cardinal points, and some mathematical knowledge. Were they the ancestors of the present Hawaiians, or of a different race that has passed away?"

He inquired of the oldest natives concerning the history of this ruin, but "they could give only vague and confused traditions in regard to it, and these were contradictory. The only point on which they agreed was that it had never been used within the memory of man." They also said there was another old structure of the same kind in Kona, whose history is lost. The language of the Sandwich Islands is so manifestly a dialect of the Malayan tongue, that the influence of the Malays must have been paramount in these islands in ancient times.

D.

DECIPHERING THE INSCRIPTIONS.

In the "Actes de la Société Philologique," Paris, for March, 1870, Mons. H. de Charencey gives some particulars of his attempt to decipher "fragments" of one or two very brief inscriptions on the bas-relief of the cross at Palenque. I know nothing of his qualifications for this work, but he appears to have studied the characters of the Maya alphabet preserved and explained by Landa. It is seen, however, that his attempt to decipher the inscriptions is a complete failure. In fact, he professes to have done no more than reproduce two or three words in Roman characters. He gives us *Hunab-ku*, *Eznab*, and *Kukulcan* as words found on the cross. *Eznab* is supposed to be the name of a month, or of a day of the week, and the others names of divinities. He finds that the characters of the inscriptions are not in all respects identical with those found in Landa, and that Landa's list, especially when tested by the inscriptions, is incomplete. There is not absolute certainty in regard to the name Kukulcan; nevertheless, M. de Charencey makes this speculative use of it:

"'The presence of the name ' Kukulcan' on the bas-relief of the cross is important in a historical point of view. The name of this demigod, which signifies ' the serpent with the quetzal plumes,' is the Maya form of the Mexican name 'Quetzalcohuatl,' which has precisely the same meaning. But we know that the name and worship of this god were brought to the high plateaus of Central America toward the ninth century of our era, consequently the bas-relief in question can not be more ancient."

This assumes that the worship of Kukulcan was never heard of by the Mayas until the Aztecs arrived in Mexico, an assumption for which there is no warrant, and which proceeds in utter disregard of facts. It was the Aztecs who had never heard of Kukulcan, or, at least, had not adopted his worship, previous to this time. The Aztecs, when they settled in Anahuac, did not impart new ideas, religion, or culture to any body; on the contrary, they received much from the civilization of their new neighbors, which was more advanced than their own. It is very certain that neither the Mayas nor the Quichés borrowed any thing from them.

We need not go back so far as the ninth century to find the time when the Aztecs adopted, or at least organized in Mexico, the worship of Kukulcan, whose name they transformed into Quetzalcohuatl. His worship did not begin with them; they did not introduce it; they found it in the country as a very ancient worship, and adopted their form of it from the people who yielded to their sway.

If M. de Charencey will inquire with a little more care, he will discover that Kukulcan was one of the very oldest personages in Central American mythology, as *Con* was one of the oldest in that of Peru. Kukulcan, sometimes as *Zamná*, was associated with almost every thing in civilization. He introduced the beginnings of civilized life, invented the art of writing, and was to the Central Americans not wholly unlike what Thoth was to the Egyptians, and Tautus, or Taut, to the Phœnicians. If the bas-relief of the cross at Palenque were half as old as his worship in Central America, it would be far more ancient than any one has supposed.

GENERAL INDEX.

[The figures in this Index refer to pages.]

Adobes used in Northern Mexico, 82; in Peru for later constructions, 241; used by Mound-Builders, 21.

Ancient history of Mexico and Central America in the old books and traditions, 197-200; Aztecs preceded by Toltecs, and Toltecs by Colhuas, 128; Colhuas the original civilizers, 198-9; they may have come from South America, 198, 200; Chichimecs the original barbarians, 198; the Colhuas first settled in Tabasco, 128; Mayas, Quichés, Tzendals, etc., originally Colhuan, 200, 202; Colhuan kingdom of Xibalba, 129; Colhuas, Toltecs, and Aztec branches of the same people, 206; such a history implied by the political condition in which the country was found, 200; theories of this old civilization considered, 195-182; it was original in America, 194-5.

Antiquity of man and civilization, 131-2, 272-3.

Antiquity of the Mexican and Central American ruins, 151-59, 184; the great forest was 450 years ago what it is now, 151; it covers an ancient seat of civilization, 95, 151, 153; Copan forgotten and mysterious before the Conquest, 152; there was a long period of history preceded by development of the civilization, 152, 153; distinct epochs traced, 155, 156; no perishable materials left in the ruins, 155-156; an extreme notion of their antiquity, 157, 159, 207; another notion makes this the "oldest civilization in the world," 159-61; Tyrians saw the old cities 3000 years ago, 162-64.

Antiquity of the Mound-Builders, 45-51; a new river terrace formed since they left, 47; decayed condition of their skeletons shows antiquity, 48-9; "primeval" forests found growing over their works, 50-1.

Astronomical monument in Southern Mexico, 122-3; at Chapultepec, 220-1; in Peru, 254; Mexican calendars, 213-15; Peruvian calendars, 226. See Telescopic Tubes.

Atlantis supposed to be an ingulfed part of America, 175-7; its destruction recorded in Egypt and related to Solon, 177-8; said to be recorded in old Central American books, 176; Proclus on remembrance of Atlantis, 178; derivation of the words Atlas, Atlantes, and Atlantic, 172; opinions relative to former existence of such land, 180-1; geological probabilities, 181; memory of war with the Atlantes preserved at Athens, 178.

Aztec civilization denied in a "New History," 207-8; facts discredit this denial, 208-9; Cortez found abundant supplies, 208, 210; found Mexican mechanics, masons, and the like, 213, 214, 215; the city of Mexico and its great temple, realities, 208, 212, 215; both described, 211-13; present remains of them, 214-15.

Aztecs, the, were less civilized than their predecessors, 221; they came from the south, 217-18; when they left Aztlan, 219; how long they had been in Mexico, 219; what they learned and borrowed of their neighbors, 220-1; did not adopt the phonetic system of writing, 221; could not have left such ruined cities as Palenque and Mitla, 221; Aztecs still found at the south, 218-19.

Balboa's hunt for Peru, 223-4.

Basques, their fishing voyages to America, 62.

Books of ancient America destroyed in Mexico and Central America by the Aztec Ytzcoatl, 189; by Spanish fanaticism, 189-9; a few of the later books saved, 189-190; some of the more important, ibid.; books of hieroglyphics in Peru, 224.

Boturini collected Mexican and Central American books, 190; misfortunes of his collection, 190-1.

Brasseur de Bourbourg on the antiquity of the Mound-Builders, 51; on their Mexican origin, 57; on their religion, 58; on the Chichimecs, 198; on Huehue Tlapalan, 201; on Nahuatl chro-

mology, 264; his "Atlantic theory," 159, 160, 171-83; he has great knowledge of American traditions and antiquities, 174; discovered the works of Ximenes and Landa's Maya alphabet, 121, 122; translated "Popol-Vuh," 122; he is unsystematic, confused, and fanciful, 102, 103.
Brereton on the wild Indians of New England, 61-5; his invented stories of their copper and flax, 64, 65.

Calendars in **Mexico**, 214-15; in Peru, 224.
Central American and Southern Mexican ruins most important, 83; their masonry and ornamentation, 123-101; a great forest covers most of them, 94, 108; had a road built into the forest in 1696, 95, 181-2; this forest covers a chief seat of the ancient civilization, 95; Chiaca-Mecallo, 124.
Cevola, "Seven Cities" of, 85-9.
Charencey, M. de, attempts to decipher an inscription, 292-3; his singular speculation concerning the worship of Kaknicab, 293.
Charnay, Désiré, his account of Mitla, 121, 122.
Chronology of the Mexican race, 202-4; of the Peruvians, 205-6.
Civilization, antiquity of, underrated, 181-2, 273.
Cloth of Mound-Builders, fragments of, 41.
Coin among the Mayacas, 271.
"Coliseum" at Copan, 113.
Columbus and the Mayas, 202-10.
Copan, its ruins situated in wild region, 111; first discovered in 1576, and were then mysterious to the natives, 93, 111; what Mr. Stephens saw there, 111, 112; what Palacios found there 300 years ago, 113, 114; the inscriptions, monoliths, and decorations, 115; seems older than Palenque, 112, 113, 125.
Copper of Lake Superior described, 43.
Coronado's conquest of "Cevola," 85, 86.
Cortez invades Mexico, 210; his progress, 210-11; well received at the city of Mexico, 211; driven from the city, 212; how the city was taken, 213-14; it was immediately rebuilt, 214; the plaza made of part of the inclosure of the great temple, 214; Cortez could not have invented the temple, 215.
Cross, the, not originally a Christian emblem, 109; vastly older than Christianity as a symbolic device, 109, 110; common in Central American ruins, 109; the assumption that it was first used as a Christian emblem has misled inquiry as to the age and origin of antiquities, 110.

Cuzco, Montesinos on its name, 227; was probably built by the Incas on the site of a ruined city of the older times, 226-7; the ruins at Cuzco, 226, 234-5.

Egyptian pyramids totally unlike those in America, 183; no resemblance between Egyptians and the Mexican race, 183.
Ethnology, American, discussed, 65-9; South Americans the oldest aborigines, 68, 69, 185; Huxley's suggestion, 69.

Gallatin, Albert, on Mound-Builders, 34.
Garcilasso partly of Inca blood, 258; not well qualified to write a history of Peru, 258-9; he began with the fable of Manco-Capac, and confined all history to the Incas, 259-61; was received as an "authority," 261; his influence has misdirected Peruvian studies, 259.
Gila, valley of, its ruins, 85.
Gold the most common metal in Peru, 224; astonishing abundance of Peruvian gold-work, 244-60; their gardens made of gold, 250; amount of gold sent from Peru to Spain, 248, 250; gold calendar found recently at Cuzco, 224.

Herrera on the buildings in Yucatan, 149.
Huehue-Tlapalan, from which the Toltecs went to Mexico, 57, 78, 201-2; supposed to be the Mississippi and Ohio valleys, 202, 203; described in old Central American books, 202; the Toltecs driven from Huehue-Tlapalan by the Chichimecs, or wild Indians, 202; it was at a distance northeast of Mexico, 201, 202; Cabrera and others on Huehue-Tlapalan, 202.
Humboldt on Phœnician symbols in America, 199; on the origin of the Aztecs, 215; on Peruvian great roads, 245; on books of hieroglyphics found in Peru, 246, 250; describes the pyramid of Papantla, 21, 22.
Huxley on American ethnology, 69.

Incas of Peru, origin of the title, 261; they represent only the last period of Peruvian history, 261; their dynasty began 500 years or less before the Conquest, 260-1; list of the Incas, 261; Manco-Capac a fable, 260-1.
Indians of North America, vain endeavors to connect them with the Mound-Builders, 62; came toward the Atlantic from the northwest, 58; the Iroquois group may have come first, 59; their distribution relative to the Algonquins, 57, 61; date of Algonquin migration estimated, 60; these Indians resemble the Koraks and Chookchees, 55, 185; they are entirely distinct from Mound-Build-

ers and Pueblos, 60, 68; their barbarism
original, 61.
"Inscription Rock," 73.
Inscriptions in Central America written
in Maya characters, 196, written perhaps in an old form of speech from
which the Maya family of dialects was
derived, 198; attempts to decipher them,
222.
Iron, names for, in ancient Peru, 248.
Israelitish theory of ancient America,
164-1.

Keweenaw Point, a copper district, 44.
Kukulcan, his worship, 190, 223.

Lake Peten in the forest, Maya settlement there, 95; Urena's road from Yucatan to the lake, 95.
Landa wrote on the Mayas of Yucatan,
121; preserved the Maya alphabet, with
explanations, 191.
Languages in Mexico and Central America, 200, 202; three groups, 215; probably not radically distinct, 205, 216; the
most important group supposed to be
Colhuan, 205.
Las Casas on Central American annalists,
151-2; what he says of the old books
and their destruction, 193.

Maize, did Indians get it from Mound-Builders? 56.
Malays, their ancient empire, 167-8; their
navigation of the Pacific, 168; spread
of their dialects, 168; came to America,
169, 170, 172; El Masdal on the Malays,
172; were not civilizers in America,
170-1; ruins of Malayan cities in Java,
165-2.
Manco-Capac a fiction of the Incas, 260-1; discarded by Montesinos and other
early Spanish writers, 261, 262.
Mandan Indians supposed Mound-Builders, 14.
Mayas first seen by Columbus, 202; their
phonetic alphabet preserved, 191; descendants of the first civilizers, 172.
Mexican cities noticed by Spaniards, 211,
215; what Montezuma said of his building material, 202.
Mexican "picture-writing" a peculiarity
of the Aztecs, 221; much inferior to the
Maya writing, 221; something like it at
Chichen-Itza, 143; Aztecs could not
have left such inscriptions as those seen
in the ruined cities, 221.
Mexican ruins in the central region, 89-92; Tulha, 82; Xochicalco, 89, 90; Papantla, 91, 92; Cholula, 90; Teotihuacan, 92; pyramids with galleries, 91;
unexplored antiquities in this region, 91.
Mining works of Mound-Builders, 42-5;

mining method of the Mound-Builders,
43; their mining tools found, 44, 46;
they left a detached mass of copper in
a mine, 43-4; antiquity of their mining works, 46, 58, 54.
Mitla, its ruins show refined skill in the
builders, 118, 121; the decorations, 121;
present state of the ruins, 117-122.
Montesinos, Fernando, explored and
studied Peru fifteen years, 261; unequaled in knowledge of its antiquities
and traditional history, 262; his means
of information, 262; how historical narratives and poems were preserved by
the amautas, 263; how literature can
be preserved by trained memory, 263-3; Homer and the Vedas, 263-4.
Montesinos on Peruvian history, 264-7;
there were three distinct periods, 264;
he rejects the Manco-Capac fable, 264;
does not begin the history with such
stories, 264; reports 64 kings in the first
period, 264; his account of the Peruvian
sovereigns, 264-5; the art of writing
existed in the older time, 265; how the
first period closed, 265; the second period, for 1000 years, a period of invasions, divisions, small states, and general decline of civilization, 264, 267; in
this period the art of writing was lost,
267; in it the 29 successors of the 64
kings were merely kings of Tampu-tocco,
266; how this period ended, 277-8; the
third period began with Rocca, the first
Inca, 261; why Montesinos has not been
duly appreciated, 263-4; his facts stand
apart from his theories, 263; probabilities favor his report of three periods,
210-1.
Montezuma on his building-material, 202.
Morgan, Lewis H., on the Indians, 59, 60,
66.
Mound-Builders, their national name unknown, 14, 51; their mound-work and
its uses, 17-19; like mound-work in
Mexico and Central America, 70, 71, 72;
their civilization, 22-29; used wood for
building material, 70, 71; their inclosures, 19-24; their works at the south,
24, 25; their principal settlements, 30,
31, 34; their border settlements, 52;
had commerce with Mexico, 13; relics
of their manufactures, 40, 41, 51; their
long stay in the country, 51-55; were
not ancestors of wild Indians, 58-61;
came from Mexico, 70; were connected
with Mexico through Texas, 73; probably were Toltecs, 74, 209-3.
Muyscas, their civilization, 271.

Nahuatl or Toltec chronology, 208-4.
Natchez Indians, were they degenerate
Mound-Builders, 63, 64.
Northmen in America, 219-30; they dis-

covered Greenland, 280; their settlements in Greenland, 280-1, 281; Biarni's constrained voyage to Massachusetts in 985 A.D., 198, 231; subsequent voyages to New England, 231-4; encounters with the Indians, 282, 238; the Norse settlements in Vinland were probably lumbering and trading establishments, 234; not people enough in Greenland and Iceland to make extensive settlements, 281; written narratives of these discoveries, 279-80.

Origin of Mexican and Central American civilization, theories of, 165-183; the "lost tribes" theory absurd, 162-1; the Malay theory untenable, 172-3; the Phoenician theory fails to explain it, 173-4; the Atlantic theory explained by Brasseur de Bourbourg not likely to be received, 182; it was an original American civilization, 181; may have begun in South America, 185, 246, 272-3.

Orton, Prof., on Peruvian antiquity, 273, 274.

Pacific islands, their antiquities, 255-22.
Palenque, Stephens's first view of, 101; this city's name unknown, 101; supposed to have been the ancient Xibalba, 102; some of its ruins described, 103-4; extent of the old city can not be determined, 95, 103; difficulties of exploration, 105, 110; the cross at Palenque, 110; aqueduct, 103.
Palmilla, its remarkable stone pyramid, 91, 92; important ruins in the forests of Palmilla and Misantla, 91.
Paper, Peruvian name of, 267; manufacture of, for writing, preserved in the second period of Peruvian history, 267.
Peruvian ancient history, 231-47.
Peruvian civilization, 241; differed from Central American, 224-5, 246; is seen in the civil and industrial organization, 247; in their agriculture, 247; in their manufactures, 247-51; their dyes, 247-8; their skill in gold-work, 242; the abundance of gold-work, 248-50; their schools of the amautas, 253, 263; their literature, 253; anciently had the art of writing, 265, 266; had names for iron, and said to have worked iron mines, 248-9.
Peruvian ruins, where found, 272, 273; they represent two periods of civilization, 236; remains on islands in Lake Titicaca, 271-3; at Tiahuanaco, 273-4; remarkable monolithic gateways, 273-4; at old Huanuco, 239-40; at Gran-Chimu, 237-8; ruins of a large and populous city, 237; Cuelap, 238; Pachacamac, 242; subterranean passage under a river, 243; the aqueduct, 242, 243; the great roads, 242-3; ruins at Cuzco, 235.

Phoenicians, or people of that race, came probably to America in very ancient times, 172, 173; decline of geographical knowledge around the Aegean after Phoenicia was subjugated, about B.C. 818, 172-3; supposed Phoenician symbols in Central America, 156; Phoenician race may have influenced Central American civilization, but did not originate it, 173, 157; Tyrians storm-driven to America, 161, 162.

Pizarro seeks Peru, 224-5; discovers the country, 225; goes to Spain for aid, 226; finally lands at Tumbez, 226; marches to Caxamalca, 229; perpetrates wholesale murder and seizes the Inca, 229; the Inca fills a room with gold for ransom, and is murdered, 229, 242.

"Popol-Vuh," an old Quiché book translated, 192; what it contains, 193; Quiché account of the creation, 193; four attempts to create men, 193-5; its mythology grew out of an older system, 193-4; kingdom of Quiché not older than 1000 A.D., 193.

Pueblos, 16, 71; Pueblo ruins, 71-90; occupied northern frontier of the Mexican race, 68, 217-19; unlike the wild Indians, 67-8.

Quichés, notices of, 192.
Quipus, Peruvian, 254-5.
Quirigua, its ruins like those of Copan, but older, 114; it is greatly decayed, 117; has inscriptions, 114.
Quito subjugated by Huayna-Capac, 223; was civilized like Peru, 270; modern traveler's remark on, 276.

Savage theory of human history, 152.
"Semi-Village Indians," 67, 68.
Serpent, figures of, 28; great serpent inclosure, 28.
Simpson, Lieut., describes a Pueblo ruin, 58, 59.
Spinning and weaving in Peru, 247; vestiges of these arts among the Mound-Builders, 41; the Mayas had textile fabrics, 209.
Squier on the Aztecs, 92; on the more southern ruins in Central America, 123, 124; on the monoliths of Copan, 112; on Central American forests, 94; on the ruins of Tiahuanaco, 234.

Telescopic tubes of the Mound-Builders, 42; silver figure of a Peruvian using such a tube, 254; such a tube on a Mexican monument, 133.

"Tennis Court" at Chichen-Itza, 142.
Titicaca Lake, its elevation above sea-level, 234.

Tlascalans, what Cortez found among them, 210; their capital, 211; aided the Spaniards, 211.
Toltecs identified with the Mound-Builders, 201–205; how they came to Mexico, 201, 202; date of their migration, 201. See Huehue Tlapalan.
Tuloom, in Yucatan, 154.

Uxmal described, 131–137; more modern than Palenque, 130; partly inhabited, perhaps, when Cortez invaded Mexico, 131, 135.

Valley of Rio Verde, its ruins, 62, 63.

Wallace, A. R., on ruins in Java, 108–9.
Welsh, the, in America, 243–7; Prince Madog's emigration, 243; his colony supposed to have been destroyed or absorbed by the Indians, 246; letter of Rev. Morgan Jones on his "travels" among the Doeg Indians who spoke Welsh, 246–7.
Whipple, Lieut., on Pueblo ruins, 78–85.
Whittlesey on the ancient mining, 40, &c.
Wilson's discoveries in Ecuador, 271–8.
Writing, phonetic, among the Mayas, 187–91; Aztec writing much ruder, 241; writing in Peru, 264–5, 267; Peruvian books of hieroglyphics, 256; such writing on a llama skin found at Lake Titicaca, 256.

Xibalba, an ancient Colhuan kingdom, where it was situated, 129; subjugated by the Toltecs, 129.
Ximenes, Father Francisco, his manuscript work on Guatemala, 191–2; his dictionary of the native tongues, 192; discovered and translated "Popol Vuh," 192.
Xochicalco, its pyramidal temple situated on an excavated and chambered hill, 89, 90.

Yucatan, its native name is Maya, 125; what is seen at Mayapan, 127, 128; the old edifices at Uxmal, 131–137; very ancient ruins at Kabah, 137–129; curious construction at Chichen-Itza, 142; remarkable remains at Ake, 144; aguadoes in Yucatan, 145, 146; subterranean reservoirs, 146; Merida built on the site of a ruined city, 126; what the Spaniards saw when they first sailed along its coast, 165, 210.

Zuni, an inhabited Pueblo described by Lieut. Whipple, 79, 80; ruins of an "old Zuni" near it, 80, 81.

THE END.

www.ingramcontent.com/pod-product-compliance
Lightning Source LLC
Chambersburg PA
CBHW032057220426
43664CB00008B/1033